SENSATIONAL

LEARNING CENTERS

Augsburg Fortress, Minneapolis

CONTENTS

Sensational Learning Centers

Editors: Beverly Riis Sperry and Eileen K. Zahn
Designer: Lecy Design
Illustrator: RKB Studios

Scripture quotations marked TEV are from Today's English Version of the Bible, copyright 1976 by the American Bible Society. Used by permission.

"Kaleidoscope of Blessings" by Robin Currie, copyright © 1990 Augsburg Fortress. "Pathways of Prayer" by Jeanne Coolahan Mueller copyright © 1984 Augsburg Publishing House. "Celebration Station" by Margaret Marcrander, copyright © 1988 Augsburg Publishing House. "Mission Expedition" by Phyllis Vos Wezeman and Colleen Aalsburg Wiessner and "Mission Stories" contributors Mary Nelson, Richard Nelson, Gerhard Reitz, Dean Peterson, William Radatz, copyright © 1989 Augsburg Fortress. "Rainbow Connection" by Jeanne Coolahan Mueller, copyright © 1981, Augsburg Publishing House.

Manufactured in U.S.A.
1 2 3 4 5 6 7 8 9 0 1 2 3 4 5 6 7 8 9

LEARNING CENTERS

Sensational Learning Centers is designed to help congregations provide fun Christian educational experiences based on specific themes. This guide contains detailed instructions for five centers: Kaleidoscope of Blessings (focused on the ways we have been blessed by God), Pathways of Prayer (prayer), Celebration Station (celebrating the good news), Mission Expedition (how we share the good news), and Rainbow Connection (living joyfully as God's people).

As you look for exciting, innovative approaches to learning, consider what learning centers can do for your program:
● complement classroom sessions by amplifying church school lessons or exploring new ones;
● provide a change of pace for leaders as well as students;
● invite interaction among students of various age levels and between students and leaders;
● emphasize learning by doing, touching, and building;
● expand students' options, helping to better meet their needs as they seek meaning for their lives through Jesus Christ.

Learning centers can be used in a variety of ways:
● on a series of Sunday mornings, for two to five sessions on one theme;
● for a special two- to three-hour evening program;
● as a resource for midweek programs of faith instruction;
● for an all-school event during school vacations;
● as a supplementary resource for your regular curriculum;
● on special Sundays in various seasons of the year or at any time you want to provide intergenerational activities.

Each center may be developed in many ways. This guide includes ideas and organizational structures for all-school and intergenerational participation. The suggestions are designed for use with students preschool through upper elementary. They can, however, be adapted so learners of all ages can enjoy them. Study closely the age-level activities listed and make the necessary adjustments so learners of all ages might be included. Be especially conscious of the adjustments if planning an intergenerational program. Use your imagination to make each center an exciting place to meet, learn, and grow.

The learning centers are places where classes gather to share, sing, look, listen, and do. These are places where children, youth, and adults can tell stories, perform with puppets, display things they have made, hang banners, and discover some of the interesting things that others have learned, all done in a context of fun.

This guide can stimulate new ideas, but people are your best resource. It is by working and learning with others that we share and grow in our faith. Involve members of your congregation and others who have a special interest in children and in activities for children. Consider working with other churches to sponsor an event together. Make the sensational learning centers true community-of-faith events.

Coordinating Your Center

Select a center coordinator. You may choose to have one person or a team of people fill this role.

The coordinating person or team should be able to:
● envision the potential of this project with enthusiasm;
● manage the many details of arranging for supplies, project materials, and other resources;
● get along well with others;
● be extremely flexible;
● be well organized;
● identify resources, such as church school curriculum, church school teachers and students, and others in the congregation and community that can provide additional activities and resources.

The development of this unique learning opportunity will require additional time, energy, and supplies. Early in the yearly planning of your Christian education program, decide on the space, schedule, and personnel that will be a part of the centers you plan to use.

Responsibilities of the Center Coordinator

The coordinator(s) might assume the following responsibilities:
● Determine with the education staff which learning areas will be offered. The education staff may decide that the activities should complement the regular classroom work, or they may choose to offer an entirely separate theme.
● Study the suggestions for the center.
● Become familiar with the learning objectives.
● Coordinate the basic plan for the particular center with the education staff.
● Survey the available spaces and select those that will be used for all-school activities. (Some specific suggestions and alternatives are included.)
● Set up a schedule and guidelines for use of the center.
● Recruit learning center guides to staff each theme area. They may be church school teachers, senior citizens, parents, teenagers, people with special talents and interests, or people who are unable to teach the

rest of the year. Contact potential leaders and describe group size, time limits, equipment available, and duties. Be sure guides are given complete information on the responsibilities involved.

● Enlist helpers for each area as needed. Groups of 10 or fewer learners generally can be handled by one person. Children in third grade and younger need additional supervision, as do larger groups or complicated activities.

● Find other people to assist in the general operation of the center. Have one unassigned person for every 20 students. These people can greet incoming students, see that they find a place to work, explain the purpose of each learning area, answer questions, and circulate throughout the area, talking informally with the students and being alert to problems that may occur. These people can help centers run much more smoothly.

● Talk with guides and teachers about the kinds of activities and displays that could take place in each theme area of the center to reinforce learning objectives.

● Gather all necessary supplies, equipment, and audiovisual materials. Make sure facilities are reserved and adequate for your needs. (Let the congregation know what is needed. People are often willing to donate items if they are aware of the needs far enough in advance.)

● Oversee the setup, decoration, and planning of activities that area leaders will carry out in the center.

● Meet with classroom teachers to familiarize them with the center.

● Assist guides by providing supplies, arranging for setup and cleanup, and handling any problems.

● Prepare an evaluation of the center for use in future years.

Setting up the Centers

Specific suggestions for site selection and setup are given in the introduction of each learning center. The following are general considerations that must be addressed in planning any of the centers.

● *Liability*. Before choosing a site, check with the pastor or the church council to address any insurance or liability issues.

● *Safety*. Be sure that areas are well defined and protected from hazards. If outdoor areas are used, provide barriers to prevent children from straying from one area to another or into areas where there is traffic. Use immovable barriers across open stairwells or at the edge of a stage area to avoid falls.

● *Accessibility*. Are there architectural features that would make this area unsuitable for people with physical disabilities? Are doorways wide enough to permit wheelchairs to enter easily? Do stairs make this area inaccessible to people with crutches or a walker? Could people who have visual disabilities be able to reach and function safely in this space?

● *Movement time*. Consider the amount of time needed to move from the class area to the center. A short walk from the church building to the park may be a welcome change and provide exercise for the participants, but if the distances are too great there will have to be some sacrifices in the learning activities to allow time for movement.

● *Relationship of activity to space*. Small spaces may be excellent choices for quiet activities and for small-group experiences. Larger spaces will be needed for more boisterous activities.

Scheduling the Center

Decide your goals for the center and who will participate. Each area activity has a suggested age level. However, activities may be adjusted to meet the interests and abilities of different age levels. Then consider the following format options.

● Schedule everyone in the learning center at the same time. This option works well if you have a small number of participants and are set up in a large area. Assign each age level (or group) to one theme area, then rotate the groups from area to area.

● Limited personnel, time, or supplies might make offering just the community activity from some of the theme areas a viable option.

● Select one or two activities in each area to be used.

● Select an activity and take it to individual classrooms if done during church school.

● Schedule each class or age-level group at different times. This allows one or more areas to be available to the class. Allow between 15 and 30 minutes for a visit.

● A small school may conduct its entire school in the learning center.

● An intergenerational center may have adults and children rotate through the areas together, with adults helping children in the activities.

● Encourage the congregation to attend an open house of the completed learning center.

KALEIDOSCOPE OF BLESSINGS

Blessed to Be a Blessing

God's people are blessed. In turn we are empowered and commissioned to be a blessing to others. The Kaleidoscope of Blessings Center provides opportunities for participants to meet and share, to learn more about the ways they have been blessed by God, and how to use their gifts to bless others. Just as a kaleidoscope displays infinite patterns of beautiful colors, so art, crafts, drama, music, cooking, and stories will provide many ways for participants to explore how they are blessed to be a blessing.

A central meeting place (Star Center) and five activity areas (Sea and Sky, Hearts and Hands, Forgiveness and Freedom, Teach and Tell, Flowers and Fields) provide opportunities to experience the five themes. Each center is developed around a particular color and has a central focus activity.

Setting up Kaleidoscope of Blessings

Your own space will determine how you set up the Kaleidoscope of Blessings. One possibility is to use a large area, such as a fellowship hall, gymnasium, large classroom, or large tent, for the entire center. In such an area, the Star Center could be literally at the center of a star. Outline the star with silver duct tape on the floor and place one activity area at each of the five points.

Successful centers can also be made in two or three smaller spaces, a separate room for each activity area, or a wide hallway. Foil strips or rows of stars can connect the activity areas to the Star Center to carry out the theme. Other alternatives include using outdoor space or making portable activity areas that can be moved from classroom to classroom.

Color plays an important role in the Kaleidoscope of Blessings learning center. Each area uses a distinctive color (blue, red, white, yellow, and green) for focus. Think of each color as you plan. Collect all kinds of items in those colors to decorate the areas. Also think about colored streamers, balloons, buttons, or stickers for staff and students. Asking guides to wear an article of clothing or a little face paint to match the center color is an easy way to enhance the visual effect.

Create and display theme posters for each of the activity areas. Each poster should feature the theme and the Bible verse for that activity area. Each area should also have its name on a sign or banner. See the description of each activity area for setup suggestions.

STAR CENTER

Star Center may be used as:
- a place where activities and schedules are explained;
- a place to share, sing, or tell stories;
- a place to pass out materials.

Star Center is the starting point. The theme of this central location is related to the blessing God gave to Abraham: to give him as many descendants as there were stars in the sky (Genesis 15:5). Hang silver stars from the ceiling or use them to cover the walls and floor. If it is possible to make this area dark, tiny Christmas lights or luminescent stars and stickers will be effective. Add a rug or blanket on the floor if you will sing or tell stories. Soft music on a tape recorder will quiet the participants as they enter.

At Star Center give each participant a star cut from silver cardboard or a cardboard star covered with aluminum foil. Create a 10" five-point star pattern for use in making the stars for each participant, as well as for the possibility of a Star Center mascot. Write the participant's name in the center of his or her star. Supply each activity area with streamers in the color for that area to attach to the points of the star. These streamers may be made of crepe paper, tissue paper cut into thin strips, or gift wrap ribbon. Attach the streamers to the participants' stars as they visit each area. At the end of the learning center, each participant's star will have five different color streamers, one hanging from each point. You may wish to attach a dowel rod to each star and have participants carry them during a closing activity.

Provide a mascot for Star Center by having a staff member dressed in a colorful robe or long dress with a crown of stars. The mascot can welcome all participants with a song or a story and chat with them informally. The star can also direct participants to the next activity area or help them add the color streamers to their stars.

Use the colors of your activity areas to organize the class schedules. List all the classes on a chart and indicate the day's assigned area with colored dots. Or make a five-section color wheel and place the class names in the color areas. Even kindergartners will know where to go on "green day."

SEA AND SKY

Theme: Blessed to Trust and Believe

Objectives:
- to trust that God provides leaders for the activities of our lives
- to believe that God as the creator of all will continue to care for creation

Bible verse: God looked at everything he had made, and he was very pleased. Genesis 1:31a TEV

Setup: This area will focus on the color blue and use several games to emphasize the theme of trust. Create an atmosphere to suggest God's creation of the world. Hang blue streamers from the ceiling. On the walls hang puffy clouds cut from light blue paper and trimmed with cotton balls. Put a blue rug or blanket on the floor. Bring in a small wading pool or fill a shallow plastic tub with water. Borrow an aquarium of fish or a pet turtle. Add a few drops of blue food coloring to water in glass jars and put them on a window sill. Print the theme and the Bible verse on a sheet of blue paper and hang it at the entrance. Invite participants to help decorate this poster with drawings and cutouts of things God has created.

All Together in Sea and Sky

Pictures of a hen and ducklings will make this story-telling time great fun. Encourage the younger children to "quack" with the baby ducklings. If you are attaching blue streamers to the silver stars made in Star Center, do it after the story.

Follow Me!

Down the path toward the pond came the mother hen. How she strutted as she led the fuzzy yellow babies out for their walk! Along they came behind her: one, two, three, four, five, six, seven baby . . . ducklings!

Ducklings! How did that happen? When the mother duck disappeared from the nest, the farmer found a hen to sit on the duck eggs. Over the days and weeks it took to hatch the eggs, the mother hen grew to care for the eggs as her own. After the babies hatched, the mother hen was as proud of them as if they were chicks. She did not seem to notice their funny webbed feet or the "quack-quack-quacking" sound that was so unchicken-like. She taught them to peck and scratch for corn and worms.

Once in a while, when they were near the pond, the baby ducklings gave the mother hen a scare by jumping into the water and paddling about. But when the sun set, they were all back home in the chicken coop, safe under the wings of the mother hen, trusting her through the night.

God, who created all things, is like the mother hen. We trust God to keep us safe.

Tell participants that in this center they will learn more about trusting God's promises.

Sea and Sky Activities

Puzzle makers (Preschool). *Materials needed: magazine pictures of things in nature, scissors, white glue, 6" squares of construction paper.*

Have participants choose a picture and glue it on the construction paper. Cut each picture into four or five pieces to make puzzles. Put the puzzle pieces into envelopes. Ask the participants to trade puzzles and allow time to put them together. Talk about how all of nature trusts its creator, God, to keep things in order.

Sea mural (Elementary). *Materials needed: blue tempera paint, scissors, mural paper, construction paper, paper towel and toilet paper tubes, thick yarn, sand, white glue, colored chalk.*

Create a seaside mural. Participants can divide the mural paper into water, shore, and sky. Color the sky area with blue chalk. Spread a thin layer of white glue on the shore area and sprinkle with sand. For waves, apply glue to a toilet paper tube, then wind thick yarn around the tube. When dry, insert a paper towel tube through the toilet paper tube and use the ends for handles. Roll the tube—as you would a rolling pin—through a shallow pan of blue tempera paint and then roll the tube horizontally across paper to create the sea. Shells and underwater plants can be made of construction paper. Point out how God can be trusted to guard the sea and its creatures.

Dress-up corner (Preschool). *Materials needed: a variety of items that identify caregivers the participants would recognize, such as toy fire fighter's hat, stethoscope, peace officer's hat or badge, and so on.*

Encourage the participants to try on the props and act out the roles that the caregivers represent. Discuss how each person is an example of the care that God provides for us.

Sailing boats (Upper elementary). *Materials needed: empty cardboard milk cartons (quart or half-gallon), 9" paper plates, markers, sharp paring knife.*

Make sailing boats to share with younger children. Follow these steps: rinse empty milk cartons with water. Using a sharp paring knife (*be sure to provide appropriate caution and adult supervision*), cut along one long corner of the carton, then diagonally across the top and the bottom of the carton, being careful not to cut the carton in half. Spread the carton open and glue the tops closed, if necessary. Cut a slit about 1" deep in the center ridge, angling it slightly away from the tops to accommodate the edge of the paper plate. Decorate the plate with rainbows and the words "Share God's Blessings." Insert the plate into the slit and the boat is ready to sail.

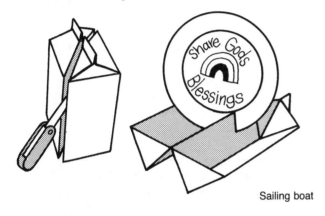

Sailing boat

Sea and sky game (All ages). *Materials needed: plastic floating toys, waterproof tape, slips of paper, shallow pan of water.*

On plastic floating toys (rubber ducks, toy boats, or plastic margarine tubs) attach names of things God created, such as a cloud, sun, star, wind, wave, fish, clam. Cover the name with waterproof tape to keep it dry. Float the toys in a shallow pan of water and have participants take turns choosing one. Each participant should act out the word written on the toy for others to guess.

Time to praise (Preschool). Join together in this praise fingerplay.

God made the stars. (*Wiggle fingers overhead.*)
God made the stars.
God made the stars,
And the sky and sea. (*Raise arms overhead, then touch ground.*)

God made the waves. (*Wiggle fingers near ground.*)
God made the waves.
God made the waves,
And the sky and sea. (*Raise arms overhead, then touch ground.*)

God made the wind. (*Wave arms overhead.*)
God made the wind.
God made the wind,
And the sky and sea. (*Raise arms overhead, then touch ground.*)

I trust the Lord. (*Raise arms.*)
I trust the Lord.
I trust the Lord
To take care of me. (*Point to self.*)

Trust plaque (Elementary). *Materials needed: 6" x 12" pieces of construction paper, 5 whole toothpicks and 12 half toothpicks per plaque, glue.*

Have the participants create a plaque that will remind them always to trust in God. Give each participant a piece of construction paper and the necessary number of toothpicks. Print "Trust" on a chalkboard or chart paper. Ask the participants to lay out the toothpicks in the same arrangement, centered on the construction paper. When all the letters are formed, show how to apply glue to one toothpick at a time, then lay the toothpick back in place on the paper. Have the participants put their names on their plaques and set them aside to dry.

A taste of sea and sky (All ages). *Materials needed: fish-shaped crackers, grape juice, paper plates, tiny party umbrellas, beach towel.*

Snack on fish-shaped crackers and grape juice. Decorating the plates with tiny party umbrellas or eating seated on a beach towel will make this snack even more fun.

Octopus obstacle course (All ages). We trust our leaders as we trust our God. Lead the participants through a series of safe obstacles, such as under tables, beneath blankets suspended between backs of chairs, and behind furniture. Hang wet strips of cloth from a doorway you pass through or have helpers stationed along the way squirt water. Have two leaders hold the ends of several long strips of blue crepe paper and wiggle them on the floor like running water. Have the participants step or jump over the "water." As a precaution, have an adult hold children's hands if they are going to jump.

HEARTS AND HANDS

Theme: Blessed to Serve and Show Mercy

Objectives:
- to experience serving others
- to identify times and ways to show mercy to others

Bible verse: I have set an example for you, so that you will do just what I have done for you. John 13:15 TEV

Setup: This area focuses on the color red and uses many cooking-related activities to emphasize the theme of service. Create a warm atmosphere of love in this center to inspire loving service to others. Cut out large and small red paper hearts and to hang from the ceiling and walls. Put a pot of red geraniums or petunias on the table. Make red paper chains to string across the entrance. Put out bowls of red fruit, like apples and strawberries, for snacks. Cover the windows with red cellophane or tissue paper. Print the theme and the Bible verse on a sheet of red paper and hang it at the entrance. Invite all participants to help decorate this poster with hearts cut from many kinds of wallpaper scraps.

All Together in Hearts and Hands

Add drama to this story by breaking an egg in a bowl, dropping a block, and almost spilling some paint when these things happen to Justin in the story. If you are attaching red streamers to the silver stars made in Star Center, do it after this story.

Not that One!

Justin heard about Jesus serving others, and he wanted to serve others too. So Justin looked for ways to help. He tried to help at home by bringing in the grocery bags. He picked up a very big one with a carton of eggs on top. "Not that one!" called his mother, right before the eggs fell out onto the ground.

Justin tried to help at school by putting away the blocks, beginning with the bottom one in the stack. "Not that one!" called his teacher, right before all the other blocks fell to the floor.

Justin tried to help at Sunday school by carrying supplies to a craft center. Justin started to pick up a big dish of red paint. "Not that one!" said the teacher, just in time. The craft leader said, "Justin, why don't you carry all the paintbrushes?"

So Justin found a way to serve others that was just right for him.

Tell participants that in the Hearts and Hands Center they will explore many ways to serve.

Hearts and Hands Activities

Set-it-yourself place mats (Preschool). *Materials needed: 12" x 18" construction paper, decorative stickers, crayons; plate, cup, fork, and spoon patterns; prayer cards, clear self-adhesive paper, white glue.*

Make patterns of a glass, plate, fork, spoon, and knife. Let the participants use these patterns to trace these shapes on construction paper to show the utensils' proper location in a table setting. Decorate the place mats with crayons and stickers. Point out that it is easier to remember how to set the table before serving food to others by using these place mats. For older participants, have them design their place mats with pictures of a way we serve others.

Copy this grace on small cards and glue it to the place mat before covering with clear self-adhesive paper.

Dear God,
We know this food is a blessing from you.
Show us the way to bless others, too!
In Jesus' name.
Amen.

Set-it-yourself place mat

Kitchen helpers (Lower elementary). *Materials needed: red felt, scissors, heart patterns of different sizes (3", 4", and 5" patterns) craft eyes or glitter, spring-type clothespins, white glue, magnetic tape.*

Show each participant how to trace hearts on felt and cut them out. Decorate the hearts with craft eyes and draw a mouth with a pen to make a face, or apply decorative glitter to the heart. Glue the heart to one side of the clothespin. Attach a strip of magnetic tape to the other. Each participant may draw a picture to clip in the magnet to take home. Suggest that these are helpful for holding recipes while cooking.

Woven hot-dish pads (Upper elementary). *Materials needed: cardboard, thick yarn, scissors, tape.*

For each participant, cut a 6" circle from cardboard. Cut six notches, evenly spaced, around the edge of the circle. Punch a hole in the center. Show participants how to tape the end of a piece of yarn to the back of the circle, above the center hole. Wrap yarn through each notch and back through the center hole. When you come to the first notch again, wrap it once more so there are two strings in that notch. Push the yarn through the center hole and tape it on the back. Tape a different color yarn to the back above the hole and bring this yarn to the front through the center hole. Begin at the center to weave under and over the yarn spokes. When you come to the two strings together in one notch, go under and over them as separate strings. Tie on more yarn as necessary, tucking the knot under the weaving. At the outer edge, bring the yarn end through a notch and tape on the back. Serving hot food will be safer with this pad.

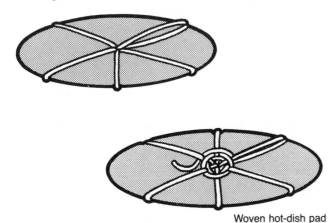

Woven hot-dish pad

"Can You Help?" game (Elementary). One person acts out a situation in which he or she needs help. When another person guesses the problem, he or she joins the first person and acts out a way to help. Then the second person acts out a new situation in which he or she needs help. Allow each participant to have a turn.

Heart mobiles (Preschool, lower elementary). *Materials needed: copies of the heart patterns used in "Kitchen Helpers" (page 8), construction paper, white glue, yarn or string, crayons, 2" x 18" strip of cardboard and two or three jingle bells for each participant.*

Participants will be reminded that we serve God with our hearts when we serve others with our hands. Trace the three heart patterns used in "Kitchen Helpers" on an 8½" x 11" piece of paper and copy enough for everyone. Ask the participants to color the three hearts and then cut them out. Then have them trace

both of their hands on construction paper and cut out the tracings. On a 2" x 18" strip of paper, have them write or stencil the words "Share God's Love." Attach this strip of paper to a strip of thin cardboard the same size. Glue this cardboard strip so it forms a circle. Assemble the mobile by hanging the hearts and hands from the circle with yarn or string. Punch holes in the tops of the hearts and the bottom of the strip. Tie the yarn to both. To make a wind chime, string two or three jingle bells together and hang them from the center of the mobile.

Diorama (Elementary, upper elementary). *Materials needed: cardboard shoe boxes, scissors, glue, crayons or markers, construction paper, fabric scraps, a Bible or Bible storybook.*

The story of the good Samaritan demonstrates the kind of servanthood that Jesus modeled. Read, or have the participants read, this story from Luke 10:25-37 or a Bible storybook.

Ask the participants to imagine the scene of the Samaritan helping the injured traveler. Encourage them to use their imaginations in drawing, cutting, and gluing figures and scenery in the box. The box should be laid on its side, with the lid removed. Make a sign to stand on the top of box reading, "Love your neighbor as yourself."

I have a dream (Elementary, upper elementary). *Materials needed: a copy of Martin Luther King, Jr.'s "I Have a Dream" speech.*

Check at a public library for the speech. Read parts of it and talk about the participants' dreams for a better world and what they could do to help their dreams come true.

Popcorn game (Preschool, lower elementary). Seat participants in a circle. One person is "It" and walks around the circle tapping the others on the head, saying "pop, pop, pop." When "It" taps a person and says "popcorn," the seated person pops up and races "It" around the circle, in the opposite direction, to the open spot. The first one there is seated. The other becomes "It" and the popping continues. We can serve others by taking turns and being good sports.

Helping heart cutouts (All ages). *Materials needed: heart-shaped cookies, icing, and sugar sprinkles or heart-shaped cookie cutter, bread, cheese or peanut butter, and raisins.*

Have participants wash their hands and then decorate the heart cookies or bread cutouts with toppings. Each participant should decorate one heart to eat and another to give to someone else. Serving others means sharing and helping.

What service? (Elementary). *Materials needed: construction paper, scissors.*

Trace hands on paper and cut out the shapes. On each hand write the name of a person in a service profession. (*Doctor, garbage collector, bagger at food store, teacher, pastor, parent.*) Put these in a basket and have the participants draw them out to imitate while others guess. At the end of the game you may want to display the "Helpers' Hands" by hanging them with clothespins on a clothesline in the Hearts and Hands Center.

FORGIVENESS AND FREEDOM

Theme: Blessed to Forgive and Show Love

Objectives:
• to acknowledge the need for God's forgiveness
• to celebrate the love God has shown us in sending Jesus for our forgiveness

Bible verse: Forgive us the wrongs we have done, as we forgive the wrongs that others have done to us. Matthew 6:12 TEV

Setup: This area will focus on the color white and use art and music activities to emphasize the theme of forgiveness. This should be a place that inspires quiet reflection as well as joyful expressions. Make the only entrance to the area be through a cardboard refrigerator box. Cut three sides of a large door in one side of the box and have the fourth side be the "hinge." Completely cut out a door the same size from the opposite side of the box so that participants walk through the "tunnel" created this way. Cover the box with white paper and let the participants sign the box with markers or crayons when they come to the center. Inside the area hang colored Christmas tree lights. Put a multicolored rug on the floor. Cover a table with a white cloth. Hang colorful paper butterflies from the ceiling. Assemble a variety of stuffed animals for hugging. Print the theme and the Bible verse on a sheet of white paper and hang it at the entrance. Invite all participants to help decorate this poster with colorful butterflies drawn with markers.

All Together in Forgiveness and Freedom

Any frowning stuffed animal or puppet can play the part of the grump in this read-aloud story. Move the grump about as if laughing at Lori and then hide it quickly when Lori forgives. If you are attaching white streamers to the silver stars made in Star Center, do it after this story.

The Visiting Grump

"And I am never coming out of my room again!" shouted Lori and slammed the door. Outside, Lori's little sister Theresa looked sadly at her father. "I said I was sorry about spilling on her yellow sweater. What else can I do?"

The girls' father shook his head. "Nothing else. Lori has decided to 'have a grump.'"

Theresa giggled. "Lori has a grump?" she asked.

Father smiled too. "A 'grump' is when you stay angry after it is time to forgive. Lori may find out her grump isn't as much fun as she thinks."

Lori heard them. "Real funny," she thought, "spilling on me and laughing about it. I'm never speaking to them again, and I'll stay here in my room forever." So there Lori stayed with her grump.

In the kitchen, spaghetti with meat sauce was cooking. Mother came home and said, "Pretty quiet in here tonight."

Lori smelled dinner and heard her mother come in. She said, "I don't care who is here or what they eat. I'm not coming out." So there Lori stayed with her grump.

Finally Mother came to Lori's door. "Are you having fun in there?" she asked.

Lori thought, "Not really." It wasn't fun being mad at everyone, and Lori was hungry. But she didn't say anything and she hung onto her grump.

Mother said, "I brought you some spaghetti, but if you are determined to stay in there with your grump, the only way to get it to you is to push it through the keyhole."

When Lori thought of her mother kneeling on the other side of the door, pushing spaghetti through the keyhole, she couldn't help but laugh. And by the time she opened the door, Lori had forgiven Theresa, the grump was gone, and Lori was happy again.

Tell the participants that in this center they will find out more about forgiveness.

Forgiveness and Freedom Activities

Butterflies (Preschool, lower elementary). *Materials needed: white construction paper, small paper plates, crayons or markers, scissors, pencils, white glue, long chenille craft stems.*

Have adults or teens help each participant trace both hands on a sheet of white construction paper. Lay that sheet on an identical plain sheet and cut around the tracings through both layers, creating four hands. Let the children color the hand tracings with crayon or marker. Fold each chenille craft stem in half and curl the ends to represent antennae. Turn the paper plate upside down and glue the chenille craft stem across the bottom of the paper plate. Glue two of the hand tracings to the right of the chenille craft stems, overlapping the palms slightly with one hand turned so the fingers point toward the front of the plate, the other with the fingers pointing toward the back. Place two hand tracings to the left of the chenille craft stem in the same manner. Bend the paper plate so the edges touch and the chenille craft stem and hands lay flat across the top. Staple these sides of the paper plate below the butterfly to form a handle. Flap the butterfly wings by moving the paper plate up and down. Say the following words as you fly the butterflies around the room. Say that butterflies are a symbol of Jesus' new life and his forgiveness that gives us new life.

Butterfly, butterfly,
Flutter by all the flowers.
How I wish I could be
Flying so high and free.

Butterfly mosaics (Elementary). *Materials needed: brightly colored tissue paper, scissors, white glue, construction paper.*

Cut the tissue paper into small squares. Have participants use markers to draw the outline of a butterfly on a piece of construction paper. Fill in the wing area by gluing on the cut pieces of paper. Like the butterfly that flies free from its cocoon, knowing that our sins are forgiven frees us to love and forgive others.

Quilt squares (All ages). *Materials needed: copies of a quilt block design, mural paper and markers* or *fabric and fabric crayons.*

Create an 8½" square quilt block design. Make copies for all the participants on 8½" x 11" paper. The blocks can be used to make a quilt mural on paper or an actual fabric quilt. For a quilt mural, have participants color a copy of the quilt block with crayons or

markers. Cut out the squares and arrange them on a bulletin board or mural paper titled "God forgives us. We live in the warmth of God's love."

To make a fabric quilt, use fabric crayons to color the design on the paper quilt square. Follow the directions on the package of fabric crayons to iron the designs onto the center of 8½" squares of plain fabric. Ask adult volunteers to sew the squares together into a quilt top and to add filling and backing. If possible, have the participants tie the finished quilt with yarn. Give the quilt to a care agency, shelter, or world relief agency. Individual quilt squares can also be made into pillows for residents of care centers.

Kaleidoscope sun catchers (All ages). *Materials needed: 7½" paper patterns, construction paper, white glue, craft knife, tissue paper in many colors.*

The everchanging colors of a kaleidoscope can help us remember the ever-unfolding blessings of God's love for us. There are two ways to make the sun catchers. Both methods require that multiple paper patterns, resembling the view through a kaleidoscope, be made prior to the session. These can be made with the same method used for paper snowflakes. For younger children, center the pattern on a 9" square of white tissue paper. Use markers to lightly color in the spaces. Make a frame from construction paper and glue the tissue paper to it. Hang in a sunny window.

Kaleidoscope sun catcher

For older participants, trace the kaleidoscope pattern onto a sheet of construction paper. Lay a second sheet of construction paper under it and use a craft knife to cut through both layers of paper as the pieces of the kaleidoscope pattern are cut and removed. (*Only adults should use craft knives.*) Working on the back of one kaleidoscope piece, glue small pieces of

Quilt square

tissue paper in place, forming a design of many colors. When all spaces are covered, glue the second kaleidoscope piece in place to cover the tissue paper edges. Attach a thread for hanging in a sunny window.

Musical free game (Preschool). *Materials needed: tape recorder, lively music on cassette, ball or beanbag.*

Play lively music on a tape recorder. Pass a ball or beanbag around the circle. When the music stops, the child holding the ball or beanbag says, "Jesus loves me. I'm forgiven and free!" For very young children you can say the verse for them: "Jesus loves (*participant's name*). (*He/she*) is forgiven and free."

Joyful noise instruments (Preschool, lower elementary). *Materials needed: markers, shoe box tops, small boxes, rubber bands, small rocks, self-adhesive paper, tape.*

Make harp-like instruments by covering a shoe box lid with self-adhesive paper or decorating it with markers. Slip five to seven rubber bands of various thickness lengthwise around the lid. Pluck the bands to play the instrument.

Make a shaker instrument by putting a handful of small rocks inside a box. Tape tightly closed. Decorate with markers or cover with self-adhesive paper. Shake to play.

Use the instruments to accompany singing favorite songs.

Reflectors (Upper elementary). *Materials needed: aluminum foil, thin, dark-colored cardboard, glue, scissors, an electric light (optional).*

Cut smooth pieces of foil into various odd shapes. Glue the shapes to the cardboard to create a reflector, being careful not to wrinkle the foil. Hold reflectors under a bright light, such as a light bulb or sunlight, and turn the cardboard at different angles until the reflected light bounces on a wall, ceiling, or floor. Create many patterns of light by gently bending the reflector. Participants may want to invent games, such as light tag, using their reflectors to "tag" others. Talk about how we reflect the light of Jesus' forgiveness to others.

TEACH AND TELL

Theme: Blessed to Give and Bear Witness

Objectives:
• to experience giving in response to God's blessings
• to practice sharing the good news of Jesus' life and salvation

Bible verse: Your light must shine before people, so that they will see the good things you do and praise your Father in heaven. Matthew 5:16b TEV

Setup: This area will focus on the color yellow and use some drama experiences to emphasize the theme of witnessing. Make this area a sunny celebration. The news is too good to hide! Place yellow balloons everywhere. Have the participants draw happy faces on them. Set bouquets of daisies and dandelions in jars. Borrow a canary to sing in a cage. Open the curtains and let the sunshine in or take this area outdoors. Print the theme and the Bible verse on a sheet of paper and hang it at the entrance. Invite participants to help decorate this poster with happy faces.

All Together in Teach and Tell

At the end of this read-aloud story you may wish to whisper the secret to each child and then shout out the good news together. If you are attaching yellow streamers to the silver stars made in Star Center, do it after this story.

Don't Keep This Secret!

All the children loved secrets. One child whispered to another, "I'm going to the zoo tomorrow." Then they would both say out loud, "Keep it a secret."

Another child whispered to a friend, "We are having a hot dog roast at our house tonight." Then they would both say out loud, "Keep it a secret."

One day the teacher had a secret. As each child came in, the teacher whispered the secret just to that person. Every child who heard it smiled.

After all the children arrived, the teacher said, "I told each of you a secret today, but it is not one that we should keep secret. The message I gave you is one we should tell everyone. So when I count to three, tell everyone this secret! One, two, three. . ."

All the children shouted at once, "Jesus loves you!"

Tell the participants that the activities in this center will help them tell others about Jesus.

Teach and Tell Activities

"My Friend" song (Preschool, lower elementary). Walk in a circle as you sing this song to the tune of "Mulberry Bush."

Let me tell you about my friend,
About my friend, about my friend.
Let me tell you about my friend.
He's your friend too. It's Jesus.

Let pairs of the participants come to the center and practice saying one sentence to each other about Jesus. That's how evangelism starts!

Wind wavers (Preschool, lower elementary). *Materials needed: wire coat hangers, clean, discarded nylon stockings or panty hose in a variety of shades, from beige to black, thread, strips of colored tissue paper, construction paper, white glue.*

Bend the wire hangers until the triangle is relatively round. Squeeze the hook together until it forms a loop handle. Cut off the leg and foot portion of the nylons. Stretch this piece over the rounded part to form a "skin" over the hoop area. Gather the open part of the stocking at the handle. Demonstrate how to glue on a smiling face from construction paper cutouts. Glue the strips of tissue paper around the face for hair. Running in the wind with these wind wavers lets the world know the happiness we feel loving Jesus and being loved by him.

Kaleidoscope bank (Elementary). *Materials needed: white writing paper, colorful tissue paper, scissors, glue, water, margarine tubs, old or inexpensive 1" wide paintbrushes, waxed paper, empty, clean cans or containers with plastic lids (such as ready-to-spread frosting or peanut cans), craft knife.*

When we share our gifts we show and tell others of our love for God and for them. A bank can help us put aside money which can be contributed to a "kaleidoscope" of worthwhile causes. Make a bank with a kaleidoscope motif by cutting a strip of white writing paper that will fit around the container chosen. Lay that strip on a piece of waxed paper. Cut colored tissue paper into small irregular pieces. Put glue into several margarine tubs and dilute the glue with a little bit of water. Using old or inexpensive paintbrushes, paint glue onto a small area of the paper strip. Lay pieces of tissue paper randomly on the glued area, then brush a thin coat of the glue mixture over the tissue paper. Continue until the entire strip is covered. While the paper is still flexible, wrap it around the container and fasten. Use a craft knife to cut a coin-size slot in each plastic lid, then put the lid on the container.

Noncompetitive musical chairs (Elementary). *Materials needed: child-sized chairs, record player and record or cassette player and tape.*

Provide one less chair than the number of participants. Select a lively song to play on the record player or cassette player. The game is played just the opposite from the usual musical chairs game. When the music stops, all participants sit down, with someone offering to share a chair with the leftover player. Remove one more chair and continue. As the number of chairs gets down to one or two, players no longer need to be sitting, but merely touching a chair. Compliment the players for their display of sharing.

Woven mobiles (Upper elementary). *Materials needed: wire coat hangers, heavy yarn or string, ½" wide construction paper strips in bright colors, markers, cross pattern, white glue.*

Guide participants in the following steps to make mobiles. First, pull a wire coat hanger into a diamond shape. Tie one end of a long piece of yarn or string to one side. Tightly wrap the string around the coat hanger, leaving space between the strands. Tie the loose end securely. Carefully weave strips of construction paper through the yarn wrap. When finished, write a witness message such as "Share God's Blessings" or "Jesus Loves Us" on a cross. Glue the cross to the weaving.

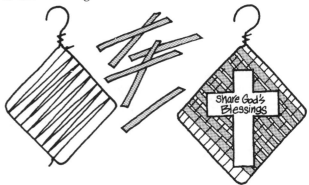

Woven mobile

Sharing blessings (All ages). Make popcorn. Show the participants a few unpopped kernels. Compare them to the fluffy popped kernels. When we know and love Jesus, we are like the popcorn—we just can't keep the good news inside. We want to burst out and share that good news with others. As the participants eat popcorn, talk about ways we can show or tell others about God's love in Jesus.

Telling the good news (Upper elementary). *Materials needed: video recording equipment.*

Let participants work together to produce a videotaped program which would be suitable for the pastor to take on a visit to a care facility or a private home that has a VCR.

List what kinds of jobs will need to be done and let everyone in the group make choices from that list. There will need to be writers, production crew, performers, and possibly prop coordinators. Get everyone involved in some way, and be sure that each one appears on the videotape in some capacity. The group may choose to dramatize a Bible story, write and read stories or poetry, display artwork, sing, dance, play an instrument, recite Bible verses, or whatever other method would convey the good news of God's love to the viewer.

FLOWERS AND FIELDS

Theme: Blessed to Hope and Receive God's Blessing

Objectives:
- to rejoice in hope
- to give thanks that we have been chosen to receive God's blessing

Bible verse: Let the children come to me. Mark 10:14 TEV

Setup: This area will focus on the color green and use some activities with nature items to emphasize the theme of hope. Let nature bloom in this area. Bring in plants of all kinds. Cut leaves of green paper to cover the walls. Frame the entrance with thick cord and attach paper leaves to look like vines. Put a green blanket or artificial grass on the floor. Borrow a turtle, lizard, or frog in an aquarium. Hang animal pictures cut from nature magazines. Print the theme and the Bible verse on a sheet of green paper and hang it at the entrance. Invite participants to help decorate this poster with drawings of flowers.

All Together in Flowers and Fields

You may wish to show a handful of sunflower seeds and peanuts when they are mentioned in the story. If you are attaching green streamers to the silver stars made at Star Center, do it after this story.

Hope for Miracles

The little brown squirrel did not waste any time. She scurried down the tree and raced for a certain spot, just to the left of the lawn chair. Her hiding place for nuts and acorns was there. I had seen her bury things there often and knew what she was after.

I also knew her treasures were gone.

A large gray squirrel had dug them up just yesterday. He was a stranger to the yard. It was a lucky guess, or his very keen nose, that helped him discover the nuts and acorns. Now they were gone. The little brown squirrel dug slightly to the left and right of her spot, then dug deeper, then went back through the dirt piled behind her. How could this be? Where were those nuts?

She scampered back up the tree, but in a flash was down again. Had she checked some chart that told her the exact location of all her treasures? Dig, look, tip her head to one side. Nothing there. Nothing there at all.

Slowly now, she went back up the tree. Her hope had been so great that everything would be where she left it.

So quietly I took a handful of sunflower seeds and a few peanuts still in the shell. I put them in the little hiding place and then went inside to watch. Would she come for them or had she given up hope of finding anything in the hole again?

Soon she scampered back and found the treats. Her head tipped to one side. She was puzzled at first. Were these the things she left? No. But she loved sunflower seeds. She ate one and then another. Then she dug everything out, rearranged things the way she wanted them, then covered them up. Now satisfied, she went darting through the grass and up the big pine tree.

When we place our hope in God sometimes wonderful things happen. And we know that the greatest miracle is God's love for us and our love for each other. Those who participate in the activities in this center will learn more about hope.

Activities for Flowers and Fields

Flowers of the field (Preschool). *Materials needed: cardboard, small squares of colored tissue paper, white glue, construction paper, green chenille craft stems, markers.*

Make cardboard patterns of a 3" circle and a flower petal 4" long. Each participant will need a circle of cardboard and six petals of yellow construction paper. Show them how to crumple the colored tissue paper and glue it onto the circle. Glue the petals around the circle to make the flower. Add the chenille craft stem for a stem. Glue the completed flower on construction paper. Help the participants write "God Is Love" on the paper with markers.

Flower of the field

Building together (Elementary). *Materials needed: modeling clay, toothpicks, paper plates.*

Experiment with making snowflake or crystallike sculptures from clay and toothpicks. Roll small balls of clay, the size of marbles. Insert toothpicks in the clay balls and form geometric shapes by connecting them. Form the sculptures on paper plates so they may be transported home. The sculptures can be reminders of God's wondrous creation, which gives us hope.

Linked together (Upper elementary). *Materials needed: cardboard patterns of the joined rings shown below, chalk, felt scraps, sharp scissors, glue.*

Make enlarged versions of the pattern below. The actual outer diameter of each circle should be 2½". The diameter of the inner circle should be 1¼". Give each participant a cardboard pattern and scraps of felt. Use chalk to trace six of the joined rings shapes onto the felt. Cut out the shapes. Fold the first shape in half, top to bottom, and glue it at the point where they touch. Slip the next piece through the glued piece and fold it in half. Continue the chain until it is long enough for a bookmark. Glue the final link closed. This bookmark can be a reminder that all God's people are linked together in the hope that comes from God's promises.

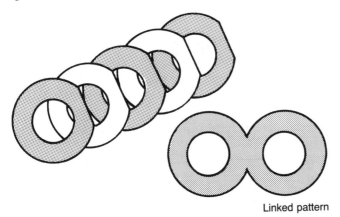

Linked pattern

Nature rubbings (All ages). *Materials needed: nature items such as leaves, petals, grass, feathers, pieces of wood (preserve nature by not picking plants still growing), white paper, magnifying glasses, old crayons without wrappers.*

Encourage participants to examine nature items with magnifying glasses. Then demonstrate how to place an item under the paper and use the side of a crayon to rub over the item. Use many items and colors to make a complete montage.

Comment that where it seems there is nothing, there is a surprise! We continually live in hope and are delightfully surprised by what God does.

"Where Are My Sheep?" game (All ages). The biblical images of Jesus as the shepherd and ourselves as his sheep are ones that fill us with hope and make us grateful to be God's child. One of these stories is in Luke 15:1-7. Read these verses to the group, then play a game involving a shepherd looking for lost sheep.

Have participants sit in a circle on the floor. Choose one child to be the shepherd. Put the shepherd in the middle of the circle on hands and knees. Blindfold the shepherd. Select two or three children to be the sheep. As they sit in their places in the circle, they intermittently begin to "baa" softly. The shepherd crawls around the circle, tapping the people thought to be the sheep. The last sheep found becomes the next shepherd.

Trail mix (All ages). Invite participants to combine raisins, dry cereal, peanuts, and chocolate chips to make a snack mix. (Check for allergies before mixing.) Divide the mixture into paper cups and enjoy the snack outdoors.

Camp out (All ages). Lay blankets on the ground outdoors or go into a dark room with flashlights. An artificial campfire or a blanket over a clothesline for a tent will add atmosphere. Read the story of Jesus blessing the children in Mark 10:13-16. Talk about how this story makes the participants feel. Name blessings for which they are thankful. Sing familiar songs, such as "Jesus Loves Me" or "What a Friend We Have in Jesus."

PATHWAYS OF PRAYER

Experience Prayer

Pathways of Prayer provides the opportunity for participants of a variety of ages to meet and share experiences that focus on prayer. Worship, songs, and art build on prayer concepts taught in the learning areas. As the participants talk and listen to God and respond to God's love with thanks and praise, they learn to make prayer an active part of their lives.

A central worship and meeting place (Joyful Junction) and five learning areas (Worship Ways, Prayer Patch, Psalm Circle, Butterfly Booth, Peacemakers' Paradise) provide activities related to prayer. Each learning area is given a subtheme on which to focus under the main theme of prayer.

Setting up Pathways of Prayer

The available facilities and your creativity will determine how you set up Pathways of Prayer. If possible, use a large area for the complete center, such as a fellowship hall, gymnasium, large classroom, or large tent. If none is available, use two or three spaces, a separate room for each theme area, or a wide hallway. Consider the use of outdoor space or making portable theme areas that can be moved from classroom to classroom.

Display a large Pathways of Prayer banner at the entrance to the center. Locate Joyful Junction near the entrance. You will find specific suggestions concerning Joyful Junction and the activity areas in the following sections.

Follow the format for scheduling found on page 4 and adapt it to your needs. Remember that your options are only limited to your creativity.

JOYFUL JUNCTION

Joyful Junction can be used as:
● a meeting place where activities and schedules are explained;
● a place for group or individual worship and prayer;
● a gathering place for sharing, group singing, or storytelling.

Joyful Junction is the crossroads of Pathways of Prayer. Place signposts pointing outward from Joyful Junction to each theme area. Make the signs by anchoring a board or broom handle in a large can or bucket of sand or concrete and attaching a piece of poster board with the name of the activity area and an arrow pointing in the direction of the area. Lay down strips of tape to form paths leading from Joyful Junction to each activity area.

Set up a simple worship center with a cross and candles. (Check local fire laws regarding the use of candles.) Arrange for music that will be sung. You may also want to have available rhythm instruments, a guitar, Autoharp, or possibly a piano.

Make vests for your activity area guides to wear. Cut a piece of nonwoven interfacing to 14" x 34" and cut a circle in the center for slipping over the guide's head. Stitch on fabric ties at the sides. The guides can write their names and the names of their activity areas on their vests with crayons or markers.

WORSHIP WAYS

Theme: Come to God in Prayer

Objectives:
● to recognize words and symbols associated with worship
● to discover places and ways to worship God

Bible verse: Worship the Lord your God and serve only him! Matthew 4:10b TEV

Setup: Paint a picture of a church on mural paper to hang in the area. Display pictures of churches and words used in worship, such as *praise, amen, hymn, pray, offering,* and *alleluia.* Make and display a colorful poster that states the theme and the Bible verse and illustrates different symbols seen in worship places, such as the cross, triangle, shell, star, flame, and dove.

Set a table to one side of the area to be used for the area's activities. Print the name of the activity area on a circular piece of poster board and hang it in a prominent place.

Community Activity

Worship banner (All ages). *Materials needed: fabric, needle and thread or sewing machine, cord, dowel, felt letters, glue gun.*

Banners carry pictures and messages that can help us worship God. Make a worship banner to hang in Joyful Junction and later in your church. (A good resource person is someone from your church's altar guild.) Cut a 3½' x 6' piece of felt, muslin, or other plain sturdy fabric. Hem the bottom and side edges or sew on decorative fringe or trim. Fold over the top edge 2" and sew it to form a casing. Insert a dowel through the casing and attach a cord for hanging. Cut letters 4" or 5" high out of felt for the words "We Worship God" (or another phrase your group chooses). With a glue gun, glue the letters onto the banner. Each participant should add one felt or fabric cutout to the banner that tells about worship, such as praying hands, a cross, the Bible, or musical notes. If you have a large group, consider making several banners.

Worship Ways Activities

Sanctuary tour (All ages). The sanctuary is one place to worship God. Talk about other places where we worship and emphasize that we can worship God anywhere. Plan a series of activities to be completed in the church sanctuary. Invite your minister to explain the meaning and use of various items in the sanctuary. Let the participants experience standing in the pulpit, sitting in the choir loft, ringing the church bell, playing a few notes on the organ or piano, looking into the baptismal font, carrying a processional cross, and looking at the minister's robe. Talk about the symbols used in your church.

Word rubbings (Elementary). *Materials needed: lightweight cardboard, glue, writing paper, crayons.*

On cardboard, print words associated with prayer or worship, such as: *amen, rejoice, praise, sing, alleluia.* There may be several words per piece of cardboard. Outline the printed words with a thick, even line of white glue. Let the glue dry. Lay the writing paper over the cardboard and gently rub the side of a crayon (without the paper wrapper) over the letters. Watch the words magically appear on the paper. Talk about the words and their meanings. Hang the word rubbings in the center.

Symbol rubbings (Preschool). *Materials needed: same as in "Word Rubbings" above.*

Use the same methods and materials as in the activity above, but substitute outlines of Christian symbols for words. Symbols might include a cross, heart, dove, Bible, and star. Talk about the symbols and their meanings. Preschoolers will want to take their rubbings home.

Christian symbol etchings (Elementary). *Materials needed: tape, aluminum foil, lightweight cardboard, liquid soap, tempera paint, pencil or nail, brush, construction paper.*

Ask the students to name some symbols they see in church and explain what the symbols represent. Some examples: the star (*guided the Wise Men to Jesus*),

dove or flame (*Holy Spirit*), triangle (*Trinity*), shell (*Baptism*), cross (*Jesus' love*), plants (*Christian growth*). To make a foil etching, tape a piece of aluminum foil to lightweight cardboard. Add three drops of liquid soap to dark-colored tempera paint. Brush the paint over the entire surface of the foil and allow it to dry. Use a pencil or nail to carefully scratch one of the symbols into the paint, allowing the foil to show through. Add a colorful construction paper frame.

Stained-glass cookies (Upper elementary). *Materials needed: ingredients as described, waxed paper, cookie sheet, crushed hard candy, oven.*

Some churches use stained-glass windows to tell Bible stories. You can create your own stained-glass cookies. To make the dough, mix 1 cup margarine, 1 cup shortening, 2 cups sugar, 2 eggs, and 2 teaspoons vanilla. Then add 5 cups flour, 1 teaspoon baking soda, and 1 teaspoon salt. Chill the dough overnight.

The next day, roll the dough on waxed paper into "snakes" and shape the snakes into stained-glass windows or symbols you might see in church. Remember to leave some open space inside the shape for the "stained glass." Place the cookies on a well-greased cookie sheet. Fill the open spaces with crushed hard candy, such as roll candy or lollipops. The bits of candy will melt and fill in the space during baking. Bake at 350 degrees for seven to eight minutes. Allow cookies to cool for five minutes before taking them off the cookie sheet.

Stole or altar cloth (Preschool). *Materials needed: fabric of your choice, scissors, fabric paints, wide paintbrush.*

Make a stole to be worn by the pastor during a worship service or an altar cloth that can be used during a service the children will attend. Choose a fabric that will be appropriate for the project. Use a paintbrush to paint fabric paint on one hand of each participant. Help the participants make a handprint on the fabric. Have a volunteer cut and set the fabric into the intended item. Arrange for the participants to present their creation to the pastor.

Quill cross (Upper elementary). *Materials needed: construction paper, quilling paper or typing paper, pencils, glue.*

Crosses help us remember to thank God for the gift of Jesus. Quilling is an art form in which thin strips of paper are coiled tightly, then stood on edge and glued onto paper. To make a quill cross, trace a cross shape on construction paper. Resource books from the church library might suggest crosses of various the church library might suggest crosses of various shapes. Curl ¼" wide by 4" long strips of quilling paper or typing paper around a pencil tip. Let the curl relax slightly so the coils are exposed, then glue the end of the curl so it doesn't unravel further. Apply glue to a small area inside the cross and place curls on the glue. Repeat the process until the entire shape is filled.

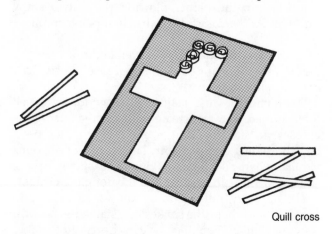

Quill cross

Creative clay crosses (Upper elementary). *Materials needed: dough (recipe below), rolling pin, table knives, paper clip, oven, acrylic paint.*

Many kinds of crosses serve as symbols of the Christian faith. These dough crosses may be hung from a cord and used as jewelry or as wall hangings.

To form the dough, mix 4 cups of flour, 2 cups of salt, and 1½" cups warm water. If you want colored dough, add 2 teaspoons oil and a few drops of food coloring.

With a rolling pin, roll dough to about ½" thickness. Use table knives to design and cut out a cross. Push an unbent paper clip partway into the top of the cross for a hanger. Bake at 325 degrees for 2½ hours. Allow crosses to cool overnight. You may decide to paint them with acrylic paint.

Exploring the worship book (Elementary, upper elementary). *Materials needed: copies of the worship book or hymnal used in your church.*

Encourage children to be active participants in the worship service by familiarizing them with the features and contents of your church's worship book or hymnal. Give them practice in finding hymns by page number. Point out the fact that most hymns are made up of stanzas. Help them find the order of worship, usually located in the front of the book. Find and read together prayers and responses that they will use in worship.

Doxology (All ages). Singing is one way to worship God. A doxology is a song of praise to God. Sing a variety of songs of praise to God. Include those from other countries.

PRAYER PATCH

Theme: Learn about Prayer

Objectives:
• to thank God for some of our many blessings, including family, friends, food, shelter, and nature
• to learn about prayer from Jesus' example and teaching

Bible verse: I will be with you always. Matthew 28:20 TEV

Setup: Using tissue paper or construction paper and tagboard, make a silhouette of praying hands. Display pictures that show people at prayer, especially children. Make and display a poster that includes the theme and the Bible verse.

Set up a table for the area's activities. Print the name of the activity area on poster board and hang it near the entrance to the area. Create a puppet theater by cutting a large square in the bottom of a carton and placing it on a table or chair.

Community Activity

Prayer squares (All ages). *Materials needed: felt squares (5" x 5"), fabric scraps, yarn, glitter, glue.*

Talk with the participants about things for which they are thankful. Provide a felt square (5" x 5" or larger) for each one. Set out fabric scraps, yarn, glitter, and glue. Each participant should design a patchwork piece that shows one thing for which she or he is thankful. Attach all of the squares to a large piece of fabric to which you have added the words, "Thank You, God." The size of the banner will depend on the number of felt squares you will include. Display the prayer square banner in the activity area.

Close the activity by reading Matthew 28:20 and praying: "Dear God, we want to thank you for (*each person names what was depicted on his or her square*). Thank you for our many blessings. Amen."

Prayer square banners could be made for prayers of petition, intercession, praise, or confession.

Prayer Patch Activities

The Lord's Prayer (All ages). Ask the children to tell about the prayer that Jesus taught us. Then offer the Lord's Prayer together.

If possible, teach the children a song version of "The Lord's Prayer." Use one that is most familiar to everyone and singable by children.

Blessings box (Elementary). *Materials needed: assortment of boxes, tempera paint, gift wrap, magazines, tape, glue.*

This activity will help participants to see God's love in family and friends. Make available an assortment of boxes ranging in size from shoe boxes to small clothing boxes. Each one chooses a box and paints the entire outside of the box with tempera paint or covers the box with gift wrap.

While the boxes dry, everyone should find pictures and words from magazines, make drawings, and write poems or stories that tell about his or her families, friends, or both. Then they can glue or tape these to all six sides of the box to create their personal blessings box. Share the boxes with others in the group.

Hand prayers (Preschool, lower elementary). *Materials needed: construction paper, crayons or markers.*

There are many people for whom we can pray. This sheet will serve as a reminder of who those people are. Have each participant place one hand on a piece of construction paper, with the fingers slightly spread apart. Trace around the hand. Have the children or adult assistants write around the drawings as shown here.

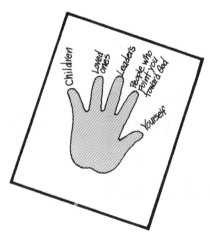

Hand prayer

Friendship pendant (Elementary, upper elementary). *Materials needed: construction paper, glue, sandpaper, shellac or nail polish, drill, string or leather thong.*

Say thank you to a friend by making a piece of jewelry for him or her. On construction paper, draw a 2" shape the friend might like (for example, a heart,

fish, or cross). Cut the shape out and make about 30 more, exactly the same, using different colors of construction paper. Glue the shapes together, one on top of the other. Let them dry for a day.

With sandpaper, sand the edges at an angle (it doesn't have to be even). Try sanding a few spots on top so different colors show through. Be patient—this will take time.

After sanding, coat the pendant with two coats of clear shellac or nail polish. When the piece has dried, have an adult use an electric drill to make a hole near the top so it can be hung on a piece of string or a leather thong.

Message mobile (Elementary). *Materials needed: colored construction paper, tagboard, markers, string or yarn, dowel.*

Identifying some words we use while praying helps us to think about different kinds of prayers. Have each participant cut six or more geometric shapes from colored construction paper or tagboard. On one side of each shape, use a marker to print a word or words we might say in a prayer. (For example: forgive me, we praise you, thank you, amen, help us, hear our prayer.) On the opposite side, draw a picture or design to illustrate the word or words you printed.

Fasten a piece of string or yarn to each shape. Hang the shapes on a dowel to form a mobile. Talk about times when you might use the words on your mobile and those on the mobiles of others.

Picture prayer (All ages). *Materials needed: typing paper, pencil, crayons, markers.*

On a piece of typing paper, draw the following shapes: the sun in the sky, a house, a tree, and a book. Make copies of this paper for each participant. Explain that prayer is a way to talk with God. You may say, "One kind of prayer is a prayer of thanksgiving. We will draw pictures of things for which to thank God." Give the following directions: "Thank God for something in the sky. Draw it in the sun shape. Thank God for something in your house. Draw it in the house shape. Thank God for something outside. Draw it in the tree shape. Thank God for something at your school. Draw it in the book shape."

Provide crayons or markers for the children to draw their responses. When you have finished, write a group thank-you prayer on newsprint, using ideas from everyone.

Prayer rainbow (Preschool, lower elementary). *Materials needed: mural paper, crayons.*

Have everyone draw a large rainbow on mural paper and use crayons to lightly color in each band. Ask them to suggest things for which they are thankful that correspond with each color in the rainbow. For instance, yellow might be sunshine or a new raincoat, while red could be a fire truck or apples. The leader or participants can use markers to draw or write their ideas on the rainbow.

When the rainbow is done, offer a thanksgiving prayer for the things listed on the prayer rainbow.

Individual cheese pretzels (Elementary). *Materials needed: margarine tubs, pretzel ingredients, oven.*

Monks in the fifth century used the shape of the pretzel as a symbol of prayer because believers often folded their arms across their chests, similar to the way the "arms" of the pretzel are crossed. Use this recipe to make pretzels. Margarine tubs make excellent mixing bowls in which each participant can mix his or her own batter. Sprinkle ½ teaspoon of yeast in 3 tablespoons of warm water. Stir to dissolve. Add ½ teaspoon of sugar, ½ cup of flour, and 2 tablespoons of grated cheddar cheese. Stir and then knead until smooth. Cut into four pieces. Roll each piece into a snake shape. Shape the snakes into pretzels. Brush with beaten egg and sprinkle with coarse ground salt. Bake on a cookie sheet at 425 degrees for 15 minutes.

"Give Thanks" table centerpiece (All ages). *Materials needed: construction paper, scissors.*

Have each person trace his or her hand on folded construction paper, making sure that the tips of the middle three fingers touch the fold. Cut out the hand tracing by cutting through both layers of paper except the fingertips. Leave the area near them uncut, creating a hinge in the paper. Leave a straight strip of

"Give Thanks" table centerpiece

paper at the wrists for a stand. Print or have available this table grace to glue to the hands:

Thanks for food to help me grow,
For family, and friends I know.
Thank you for the world I see,
Thank you, God, for loving me.

Encourage the children to place the centerpiece on their kitchen tables and to say the grace at mealtimes.

PSALM CIRCLE

Theme: Respond to God's Love and Goodness

Objectives:
• to explore the variety of feelings expressed in the psalms
• to recognize that prayer is one response to God's care and concern

Bible verse: I will praise you, Lord, with all my heart; I will tell of all the wonderful things you have done. Psalm 9:1 TEV

Setup: Decorate the area with a variety of pictures that expresses feelings such as joy, surprise, anger, and sadness. Create and display a poster featuring the theme and the Bible verse. Prepare the background for a bulletin board with the title "We're All Different, But God Loves Us All the Same."

Place a table within the center for activities. Print the name of the activity area on a circular sign and display it at the entrance to the area.

Community Activity

Praise procession (All ages). Schedule a time when all of the participants can come together for a procession to praise God. Have them bring the musical instruments made in this center. Process to a favorite song, singing praises to God.

Psalm Circle Activities

Praise instruments (All ages). *Materials needed: coffee cans, oatmeal boxes, heavy paper, paper plates, pebbles, juice can, construction paper, table-tennis ball, rice, thin 8" dowel, colored markers, sandpaper, two small blocks of wood.*

Make simple musical instruments to use in "Praise Procession" and when singing songs in Joyful Junction. Make a drum by covering a coffee can or oatmeal box with heavy paper. Make a tambourine with two paper plates and pebbles. Seal the pebbles inside the plates by stapling the plates face-to-face. Decorate the outside of the plates. Make a shaker by putting pebbles inside a juice can, taping the can closed, and covering the can with construction paper. Another type of shaker can be made by punching a small hole through opposite sides of a table-tennis ball and inserting several grains of rice through the hole. Then inset a thin dowel 8" long through the holes. Wrap tape around the dowel above and below the ball to hold it in place, and decorate the ball with markers. Make sand blocks by tacking sandpaper around two small blocks of wood.

Friendship circles (Elementary). *Materials needed: large paper plate, construction paper, glue, markers.*

God made each of us with different physical features, feelings, and abilities. Make friendship circles to bring out interesting facts about the participants and to point out how everyone is unique in some way. Take a large paper plate or circle cut from construction paper, and draw a 2" circle in its center. Have each participant draw a self-portrait or glue a photo of herself or himself in the circle. Divide the rest of the large circle into eight wedges, like a pie. Write a phrase in each section that the participants can finish with some information about themselves. Some starter phrases: "If I could be anyone in the world, I'd choose to be," "The most dangerous thing I've ever done is," "The feeling I have most of the time is," "What I'd most like to have is" "Recently I learned that," "The neatest thing about me is," or "What I would most like to do today is." When they have finished, the students can share their circles and put them on the bulletin board suggested in "Setup."

Psalm verses (Upper elementary). *Materials needed: a copy of "Psalm Circle" (below) for each person, pencil, Bible.*

Make an enlarged version of the following activity for each of the participants:

Psalm Circle

1. Psalm 107:1   Give thanks to the Lord, because he is good:

_____

2. Psalm 66:1   Praise God with shouts of joy, all people!

_____

3. Psalm 23:1   The Lord is my shepherd;

_____

4. Psalm 145:1   I will proclaim your greatness, my God and king;

_____

5. Psalm 46:1   God is our shelter and strength,

_____

_____

6. Psalm 100:1   Sing to the Lord, all the world!

_____

_____

The participants may work individually or in pairs using a Today's English Version Bible to look up each psalm listed on the sheet and complete the verse. Help those who have difficulty finding the verses. When the participants have finished, choose one of the psalms to read as a litany, dividing into two groups to read alternate verses.

"God Loves Me" pennant (Preschool, lower elementary). *Materials needed: construction paper or felt, scissors, markers, glue, dowel.*

These pennants can be made of either felt or construction paper, and they can be used in "Praise Procession" (see page 20). Cut whatever material you choose into triangular pennants about 12" long. Print "God Loves Me" on chart paper for the participants to copy onto the pennant. Staple or glue a dowel along the side of the pennant so it can be waved in the procession.

Prayer poll (Upper elementary). *Materials needed: typing or notebook paper, pencils or pens.*

Individual prayer practices vary widely. Children's prayer habits are often influenced by the traditions of their families. Help the participants look at their own prayer lives by taking a secret poll. Give each participant a sheet of paper and a pen or pencil. Have them divide the sheet into three vertical columns. Write the following on a chalkboard or chart paper and ask the participants to use them as headings for the three columns: "Usually," "Once in a While," "Never." Number from 1-10 down the left edge of the paper.

Tell the participants that you will read 10 statements about prayer. Ask that they respond honestly to each statement by putting a check mark under the column that best describes their prayer practices. Remind them that this is a private matter and that no one else will know how they answered. Read each of the following statements, pausing after each one to allow time for everyone to mark his or her sheet.

1. I pray before meals.
2. I pray when I wake up in the morning.
3. I pray before bedtime.

4. I pray at church.
5. I pray when I'm alone.
6. I pray for others.
7. I pray when I'm in trouble.
8. I pray when I want to say "thank you" to God.
9. I pray when I want God to give me something.
10. I pray when I'm sick or hurt.

Encourage the participants to look at their overall pattern and think about what they would do the same and what they might want to do differently. Be sure to use this exercise as an opportunity to encourage and enlighten, not to compare or form value judgments.

Body collage (Elementary). *Materials needed: mural paper, scissors, magazines, glue, markers.*

Help the participants use a Bible to locate and read Psalm 30:11-12. On a large piece of mural paper trace and cut out an outline of one person's body. Then have everyone cut out magazine pictures or make construction paper eyes, lips, ears, heart, hands, and feet to glue to the body. Talk about how we can use all of our body to praise God. Display the collage.

Psalm 23 diorama (Elementary). *Materials needed: shoe boxes (lids removed), construction paper, glue, colored paper, chenille craft stems, pebbles, foil, cotton balls.*

Read aloud Psalm 23 and then help the students create a diorama to illustrate the psalm. Students may work in small groups. Paint or cover the exterior of a shoe box with construction paper. Cut background scenery from colored paper and glue it to the interior of the box. Use paper, chenille craft stems, pebbles, foil, and cotton balls to make figures to glue inside the box.

We thank you (Preschool). Use this finger play with young children.

We thank you, God, for sunshine bright, (*arms up, fingers touching to make sun*)
For birds that sing at morning light, (*arms outstretched like birds flying*)
For happy children everywhere, (*clap hands lightly*)
And for God's daily, loving care. (*Head bowed and hands folded.*)

BUTTERFLY BOOTH

Theme: Ask for Daily Needs

Objectives:
● to experience God's love through natural wonders
● to pray for daily needs and to thank God for blessings

Bible verse: For all things were created by him, and all things exist through him and for him. Romans 11:36a TEV

Setup: Secure a tree branch firmly in a bucket of sand to make a "butterfly bush." Decorate the bush with the various kinds of butterflies described on page 24. Add the children's butterflies as they are made. Suspend a large tagboard and tissue paper butterfly silhouette over the area. Mount and display nature posters and pictures from magazines. Set up a table for the area activities. Create a poster displaying the theme and the Bible verse. Display the name of the activity area on a sign near the entrance to the area.

Community Activity

Creation collage (All ages). *Materials needed: blue mural paper, green construction paper, markers, paper egg cartons, tempera paint, chenille craft stems, crayons, black, brown, or gray pom-poms, string, orange, red, and yellow tissue paper, glue, brush, cupcake papers, glitter, yarn, glue.*

All of the participants can work to make a creation collage to hang in the theme area or in the church sanctuary to remind worshipers to praise God for creation.

To make the collage background, hang up a large piece of blue mural paper; fringe green construction paper for grass. With a marker, title the paper "All Things Give Glory to God." Each group that visits the theme area will create one nature item to add to the collage. Some suggestions are:

Egg-carton caterpillars. Cut off a row of six segments from a paper egg carton and paint them green. Use crayons or markers to draw on eyes. Poke pieces of chenille craft stems in the carton for feelers and legs.

Pom-pom spiders. Cut out felt eyes and glue them onto a black, brown, or gray pom-pom. Tie a piece of string around the body for a spinning thread.

Tissue sun. Tear pieces of orange, yellow, and red tissue paper. Use glue thinned with water and a brush to apply the pieces to the collage background in a sun shape.

Cupcake flowers. Decorate cupcake papers with crayon designs, glitter, yarn, or paint to look like flowers. Glue them to the mural paper and attach yarn or chenille craft stems to represent flower stems.

After a group has added its item to the collage, offer this prayer: "Creator God, we thank you for the wonders of your creation: the blue sky, the warm sunshine, flowers that smell so sweet, birds that fly in the sky, animals and insects that crawl everywhere. Thank you for making such a wonderful world. Help us to care for it. Amen."

Butterfly Booth Activities

Sand candles (Upper elementary). *Materials needed: plastic dishpans, damp sand, paraffin or old candles, stove or hot plate, crayon bits, candlewick, pencil.*

Put several inches of damp sand in each dishpan. Use your fingers to scoop out a hole in the sand in the shape that you want your candle to be. With an adult in charge, melt paraffin or old candles; add bits of crayon for color. Tie a length of candlewick to a pencil and suspend it in the middle of the sand mold. Under adult supervision, pour the melted paraffin into the mold. When the wax is cool, remove the candle from the sand. Leave some of the sand clinging to the outside of the candle. Light the candle during a worship time at Joyful Junction or in your classroom, if regulations permit.

Fruit leathers (Elementary). *Materials needed: blender, assortment of fruits, plastic wrap, cooking oil, cookie sheet, airtight container.*

With adult supervision, use a blender to puree apricots, peaches, apples, bananas, or another fruit. Pour the puree onto oiled plastic wrap that has been taped to a cookie sheet. Spread the puree to ¼" thickness. Dry it in the sun, a dehydrator, or a 200 degree oven for 4–6 hours. Roll the dried fruit and plastic wrap together and store it in an airtight container until you use it for a snack.

Sweet potato vine (All ages). *Materials needed: sweet potatoes, toothpicks, clear glass or plastic jars or containers, water.*

Insert toothpicks at four points around the middle of the sweet potato. Rest the toothpicks on the rim of the container so that half of the sweet potato is inside the container and half is above the rim. Add water to the container to cover the bottom tip of the sweet potato. Instruct the participants to place the plant near a window at home and maintain the water level. The water should be changed from time to time. A vine will sprout from the top of the sweet potato and will grow to a length of several feet.

Sun fade pictures (All ages). *Materials needed: dark-colored construction paper.*

Take a short nature walk and collect nature objects (twigs, grass, seeds, leaves, flowers). Arrange the objects in an interesting pattern on a sheet of dark-colored construction paper. Place the paper in bright sunshine for several hours. The paper will fade, leaving a silhouette of the objects. If a nature walk is not possible, have several objects available for participants to use. A bright lamp can be used in place of sunshine to fade the paper.

Echo pantomime (Preschool, lower elementary). The story of Jesus feeding the 5000 (John 6:1-13) teaches us to trust God to provide for our daily needs. In this echo pantomime the teacher tells the story and does the action, sentence by sentence, and the participants say and do everything the teacher does.

My name is Philip. (*Stand straight, point thumb to chest.*) I am a disciple who followed Jesus. (*Walk in place.*) One day we walked up a hill. (*Walk in slow, climbing motion.*) When we stopped, I was tired. (*Droop shoulders and sigh.*) I was happy to sit down. (*Sit on floor.*) We looked around. (*Hold hand above eyes and look around.*) The hill was filled with people who wanted to see Jesus. (*Move arms out wide.*) I wanted to rest. (*Rest head on palms.*) But Jesus came over to me. (*Stand.*) Jesus wanted to know where we could get food to feed everyone. (*Pat stomach.*) I didn't know what to do. (*Arms down, palms forward, shake head.*) It would take 200 coins to buy enough food. (*Hold up two fingers.*) I wanted to send everyone home. (*Move hands as if pushing away.*) A boy in the crowd walked up. (*Slap one thigh, then the other.*) Jesus looked at the boy. (*Turn head to side.*) The boy had two fish and five pieces of bread. (*Hold up two fingers and five fingers.*) That would not be enough to feed everyone. (*Shake head no.*) Jesus took the bread and fish in his hands. (*Hold out hands with palms up.*) Jesus prayed to thank God for the food. (*Bow head and fold hands.*) I helped pass out food to the people. (*Extend hands forward.*) I was surprised. (*Eyes wide open, hands in front of face.*) There was enough food for everyone. (*Extend arms out wide.*) When everyone finished eating (*move hand to mouth*), I helped pick up the food that was left. (*Reach to floor with hand.*) So my friends (*point forward*) remember this (*point to forehead*): Trust in Jesus to provide for you. (*Fold arms across chest.*)

Picture pins (Upper elementary). *Materials needed: plastic teaspoons, plaster of paris, tempera or acrylic paint, paintbrushes, small safety pins, spray shellac.*

To make the picture pin, mix the plaster according to the directions on the package. Pour it into a teaspoon and gently place the back of a safety pin into the plaster. Be sure to place the pin so that it can be opened and closed. Hold the pin in the correct position until the plaster has hardened.

After the plaster dries, carefully remove it from the teaspoon. Paint the front of the pin with a nature design such as a ladybug, bee, flower, or leaf. When the paint is dry, spray it with shellac. Participants may give the pins to members of their families.

Butterfly bush (All ages). Besides being one of God's creations, the butterfly is a symbol of hope and new life in Christ. Make several of the following kinds of butterflies to hang on the butterfly bush in the area. While the participants are making butterflies, you could read aloud from the book *Hope for the Flowers* by Trina Paulus (New York: Paulist Press, 1972).

Clothespin butterflies. Push a 6" x 8" piece of colored tissue paper or nylon net into a wooden clothespin (not the spring type). Use markers to decorate the clothespin to look like a butterfly's body. Wrap a chenille craft stem around the top of the clothespin for the butterfly's feelers.

Waxed-paper butterflies. Give each participant two pieces of waxed paper, old crayons, a blunt scissors or table knife, and a piece of string. Shave several colors of crayons onto one piece of waxed paper. Cover the shavings with the other piece of waxed paper. Lay several layers of newspaper under and over the waxed paper and press with a warm (not hot) iron to melt the shavings. When the waxed paper cools, cut a butterfly shape from the colored area. Punch a hole in the butterfly and hang it on the butterfly bush with the string.

Wire butterflies (Elementary, upper elementary). *Materials needed: thin insulated wire (coated with colored plastic).*

Fashion butterfly shapes from thin wire. Bend wire with colored insulation into the shape desired.

Bird feeder (All ages). *Materials needed: pinecones or corncobs, peanut butter, birdseed, shallow pan, yarn or string, plastic wrap.*

Feed some of God's most beautiful creatures by making bird feeders that can be hung from a tree, bush, or an outdoor railing.

Smear peanut butter on a pinecone or corncob. Place birdseed in a shallow pan and roll the coated item in it. Attach a piece of string or yarn for a hanger. Wrap the finished bird feeder in plastic wrap for the trip home.

Thanksgiving canon (Elementary). Introduce a well-known prayer and the practice of responsive reading. Print the prayer on a chalkboard or chart paper. Put a star in front of the second, fourth, and sixth lines.

For all your goodness, Lord,
We give you thanks.
Thanks for the food we eat,
And for the friends we meet;
For each new day we greet,
We give you thanks.

Divide the group in half and assign one group lines one, three, and five, and the other group the starred lines. Try having the groups stand facing each other as they read.

Peacemakers' Paradise

Theme: Living as Peacemakers

Objectives:
● to focus on words and actions that teach us to be peacemakers
● to share God's love and forgiveness with others

Bible verse: And now I give you a new commandment: love one another. John 13:34a TEV

Setup: To suggest the idea of paradise, bring in large potted plants to decorate the area. The focal point will be an abstract sculpture of paper doves made by the participants. To make the sculpture's base, secure a branch in a pail of sand. Design and display a poster featuring the theme and the Bible verse. Hang a large tissue paper and tagboard dove silhouette above the area. Print the name of the activity area on a sign and display it near the entrance. Arrange a table or work area for the activities.

Community Activity
Dove sculpture. (Preschool, lower elementary). *Materials needed: white construction paper, cardboard patterns, pencils, scissors, string.*

Make white paper doves, the symbol of peace, to create a sculpture. Provide enlarged versions of a dove similar to the one shown here. Have the children trace and cut out the doves. Hang the doves from the branches with string.

Dove pattern

(Elementary, upper elementary). *Materials needed: 6"
squares of white writing paper, string.*
Take older students step by step through these instructions for folding a paper dove.

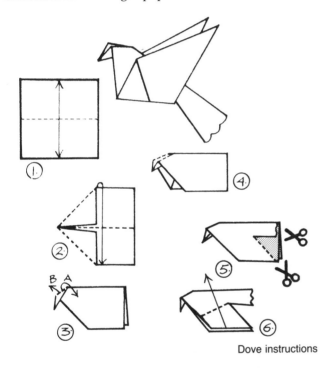

Dove instructions

After a group has made and hung its paper doves,
gather together and offer this prayer: "Loving God,
we don't always treat other people with kindness and
concern. Help us to follow Jesus' example by sharing
with others and being loving and kind to everyone.
Teach us to become peacemakers. Amen."

Peacemakers' Paradise Activities

Peacemakers' mobile (Elementary). *Materials needed:
construction paper, yarn, scissors, tagboard.*

Talk about things we can do to be peacemakers
(*pray, love, forgive, share, help*). Make a mobile to be a
reminder of these things. Cut a rectangle, heart, triangle, and circle from colored construction paper.
Print words that describe how we should act as peacemakers on each shape. Attach mobile pieces together
with yarn. Suspend the shapes from a piece of tagboard labeled "Peacemakers."

"Follow Jesus" footprints (Preschool). *Materials needed: tempera paint, shallow pan or dishpan, 12" x 18" construction paper, markers, warm soapy water, towel, newspaper or plastic cloth.*

Mix thick tempera paint in a shallow pan or dish
tub. Give the participants a piece of 12" x 18" construction paper. Have them dip their bare feet into
the paint and print their footprints on the paper. Use
a marker to write the words "Follow Jesus" on the
paper. Have a bucket of warm soapy water and towels
available for cleanup. This is a good project to do
outside; cover the area with newspapers or a plastic
cloth.

Sachets to share (Elementary). *Materials needed: cloves,
cinnamon sticks, pine needles, allspice, orange peel, 6"
squares of cotton or sheer fabric, ribbon.*

Mix cloves, cinnamon sticks, pine needles or cones,
allspice, or orange peel to make a spice sachet. Wrap
the spices in 6" squares cut from cotton or sheer fabric;
tie with a ribbon.

Spices are often mentioned in the Bible. They were
used to make ointments, anointing oils, and expensive
gifts. Have the participants think of someone with a
special need with whom they could share their sachets
as a sign of love and concern.

Bee-attitudes (Elementary). *Materials needed: paper
plate, pen, construction paper, markers, paper fasteners.*

Through the Beatitudes, Jesus taught us how we,
as peacemakers, are to act. Read Matthew 5:1-11 to
the group and then make a beatitude wheel together.

Give each participant a paper plate. Divide the plate
into eight sections and write one of these words or
phrases in each: generous, loving, honest, obedient,
humble, peacemaker, merciful, pure in heart.

Make a bee from construction paper and markers.
Attach the bee in the middle of the plate with a paper
fastener. The bee spins and points to ways we can be
God's peacemakers.

Love in action (Elementary). Ask the participants to
think of ways they could help another person. Call
on one participant to silently act out a helping situation. The other participants must guess what the
actor is doing. The first one to guess correctly acts out
a different way to help. Allow each learner to have a
turn, but do not force anyone to do so.

Glue batik peace hanging (Upper elementary). *Materials needed: 12" x 18" piece of unbleached muslin, glue, liquid fabric dye, rubber bands, yarn or twine hanger.*

Help participants make a simple symbol or slogan that conveys a message of peace, such as people holding hands, a dove, or a cross inside a heart. On a 12" x 18" piece of unbleached muslin, show the participants how to outline their design with glue from a squeeze bottle. Allow the glue to dry thoroughly, then dye the fabric in liquid fabric dye. Try tie-dying the muslin by bunching small areas of fabric and securing the bunches with rubber bands. Hang it on a clothesline to dry.

When dry, pick off the dried glue and the batiked design will be seen. Fringe the edges of the material and add a yarn or twine hanger.

Pass the peace (All ages). *Shalom* is a Hebrew word used as a greeting and as a farewell. The closest translation in English is "peace."

If you have the music, teach the Israeli round "Shalom Chaverim" (pronounced shah-LOHM ha-vay-REEM). As a group, stand in a circle while you sing the song and then pass the peace; have everyone hold hands and then give the participant next to you a light hand squeeze as you tell him or her "shalom." The participant passes the squeeze and the shalom on to the next person and so on. The song "Kum Ba Yah" could also be used. This means "Come by here" and asks God to be present.

CELEBRATION STATION

God's People Share Joy

The good news of God's love is cause for celebration and joy in the life of God's people. Not only can God's people celebrate in worship with fellow believers, but they can also celebrate through daily witnessing in their families, neighborhoods, and communities. Wherever they are and whatever they do, God's people reflect the confidence and trust that God loves them and walks with them in their daily lives. This is certainly cause for celebration!

A central meeting place (Community Hall) and five activity areas (Good News Place, Creation Station, Home Court, Praise Place, and World View) focus on celebrating God's love in all aspects of daily life.

Setting up Celebration Station

The available facilities and your creativity will determine how you set up Celebration Station. If possible, use a large area for the complete center, such as a fellowship hall, gymnasium, large classroom, or large tent. If none is available, use two or three spaces, a separate room for each activity area, or a wide hallway. Consider using outdoor space or making portable activity areas that can be moved from classroom to classroom.

The overall theme for this center is one of celebration. Use balloons, banners, and streamers to decorate the entire learning center. Display a large Celebration Station banner at the entrance to the center. Locate Community Hall near the entrance. You will find specific suggestions concerning Community Hall and the activity areas in the following sections.

Follow the format for scheduling found on page 4 and adapt it to your needs.

COMMUNITY HALL

Community Hall may be used as:
- a place where activities and schedules are explained;
- a place to share, sing, or tell stories;
- a place to pass out materials or have snacks together.

Community Hall is where we begin our celebration. Together we rejoice in all that God's love means for our daily lives, and then we go out into the world around us and witness God's love to others. A simple procedure to help the students understand this concept might be to have a short prayer or favorite song before each session. Have the participants stand in a circle, holding hands, as a demonstration of *community*. Then proceed to the activity areas.

Identify the location of Community Hall with a prominent sign. Set up a simple gathering place, with an area rug for storytelling, singing, or snacking. On a table, set out a cross and candles, songbooks, a record or tape player, and rhythm instruments for worship time. Post a "Disciple Departure" chalkboard for displaying the class schedules for the day.

GOOD NEWS PLACE

Theme: God So Loved the World

Objectives:
- to celebrate God's love as revealed in the Bible, God's Word, and in Jesus Christ, God's Son
- to see that God's love and care through Jesus are for all people

Bible verse: We know that the Son of God has come and has given us understanding, so that we know the true God. 1 John 5:20a TEV

Setup: Make a large poster to identify this as the Good News Place. Create another poster stating the theme for this area. Set up a manger scene or ask to use your church's manger scene, if possible. Bring in straw or dried grass to lay on the floor or ground around the manger. Hammer together some boards to make a simple stable or use large cardboard boxes painted to resemble boards. Cut out and paint cardboard shapes to make animals such as a donkey, some sheep, and a cow. Hang a dark blue paper mural on two sides of the manger scene. Draw a hillside landscape against the night sky (the dark blue paper) by using brown or green markers or paint. The mural will be completed in the community activity. Print the Bible verse on a sheet of manila paper and roll the paper from each end toward the middle to resemble a scroll.

Community Activity

Starry night mural (All ages). *Materials needed: dark blue paper (see "Setup"), sponges or foam shoe inserts, silver and white paint.*

Tell the participants that the shepherds were watching over their sheep in the fields when God sent angels to bring the good news to them: Jesus was born for them and for all people. Have the participants complete the mural by cutting sponges or foam shoe inserts into the shapes of stars, sheep, and angels. They can dip the stars into silver paint and the sheep and angels into white paint to print on the mural.

Good News Place Activities

Action poem (Preschool). Read the following action rhyme aloud and have the participants repeat the words and do the actions:

Christmas Is . . .
Christmas is love. (*Hug yourself.*)
Christmas is joy. (*Raise arms in the air.*)
Christmas is the birth (*cradle arms*)
of a baby boy. (*Rock cradled arms.*)
His name is Jesus.

Christmas is sharing (*extend open hands*)
peace and good news. (*Shake hands with neighbor.*)
Yes, God gave a gift (*Point up*)
to me (*point to yourself*) and to you. (*Point to neighbor.*)
His name is Jesus.

Nutshell Bible (Lower elementary). *Materials needed: Bible, unbroken walnut shell or piece of clay, 1½" x 10" strip of paper, transparent tape, glue.*

Share with the participants that John 3:16 is often called "the gospel in a nutshell." This means that it tells just about everything we need to know about who Jesus is and what God has done for us. Read the Bible verse aloud, then have the participants say it together. Give each participant an unbroken walnut shell or a piece of clay she or he can form into the shape of a shell. Also provide a 1½" x 10" strip of paper for each person. Fold the paper, accordion style, into ½" segments. Print one or two words of John 3:16 on each segment of the paper. Hinge the two halves of the walnut shell with a strip of transparent tape, or the participants can mold the shell together if they are using clay. Glue the bottom of the verse strip inside one half of the shell and refold the paper to fit inside. Carefully close the shell. Have the participants share the message in their nutshell Bibles with others.

Nutshell Bible

Scrolls (Upper elementary). *Materials needed: bread dough, toothpicks, table knives, two 10" dowels per scroll, waxed paper, plastic bags, oven (optional).*

Tell the participants that the Bible has not always looked like the ones with which we are familiar. The early writers wrote God's words on rolls of paper or dried animal skins known as scrolls. If possible, have a picture of a scroll to display. Make bread dough from 2 cups of flour, ½ cup salt, and ¾ cup water. Mix and knead the dough until it is the consistency of pie crust dough. Add water by drops if necessary. This recipe should make five or six scrolls. If more dough is needed, make it in batches rather than doubling the recipe. Store the dough in plastic bags until it is used.

Roll out a ball of dough to ¼" thick on a floured surface such as waxed paper. With a table knife, cut a rectangle about 6" x 8". Place a 10" dowel about ¼" from each of the narrow ends and roll the ends of the dough toward the middle. Leave a portion of the dough unrolled in the middle so that a Bible phrase such as part of the prophecy from Micah 5:2-5a or Isaiah 9:6-7 may be scratched in the surface of the dough with a toothpick. A small ball of dough may be pushed on each end of the dowel sticks. Bake in a 200 degree oven for several hours or dry overnight on the waxed paper. Help the participants see that God's words of promise recorded in the Bible were fulfilled through Jesus, God's Son.

Chrismons (Upper elementary). *Materials needed: tagboard, pencil, clean white plastic foam trays used for baked goods, newspapers, glue, gold glitter, gold ribbon.*

These traditional gold and white Christian symbols are used to decorate many homes and Christmas trees. Draw on tagboard and cut out simple patterns for a fish, butterfly, cross, star, crown, and shell. Place the patterns on pieces of the white plastic foam, trace around them, then cut them out. Place the shapes on newspaper, spread a thin line of glue along the outside edges of the shape and sprinkle on gold glitter. Shake off the extra glitter after the glue has set for a few minutes. Make a small hole in the top of the Chrismon and tie a piece of gold ribbon through it to form a hanger. Encourage the participants to save their Chrismons and use them at Christmas this year.

Frame drama (Upper elementary). *Materials needed: Bible story costumes, simple props, instant-developing camera and film, tagboard.*

Choose a familiar Bible story to act out, such as the story of Jesus' birth from Luke 2:8-20. Use costumes and simple props. Divide the story into several recognizable scenes. Each scene should look like the action was frozen or captured in a still photograph and framed. Explain what is happening in each scene, then let the students decide on the positions and expressions they will use to depict their scene. Share the story with someone, or use an instant-developing camera to take a snapshot of each frame. Arrange the frames to tell the story and place them on display. Add a printed dialogue for each frame.

Who am I? (Lower elementary). *Materials needed: index cards.*

Print the names of Bible characters such as Mary, Joseph, the shepherds, the angels, and baby Jesus on index cards. Have each participant select a card and use gestures and actions (without words) to act out that Bible person. The others will guess who the person is.

Straw star mobile (Upper elementary). *Materials needed: straw or colored drinking straws, scissors, red string.*

Make this straw star ornament mobile as a reminder of God's gift of Jesus, born for all people. Collect straw or colored, thin paper drinking straws, and cut them into 6" lengths. Make sure each participant has five 6" straws. Tie the straws together with red string as shown here. Make a mobile by tying the stars as shown.

Straw star mobile

"God's Love" mural (All ages). *Materials needed: large sheet of newsprint, markers or crayons, newspapers.*

Print on the newsprint in large letters, "God's Love Is for All." As each group of participants comes to the center, remind them that God sent Jesus as a gift to *all* people. Help them identify themselves as part of that group by drawing their faces and putting their names on the newsprint, along with all the other participants. If markers are being used, put newspapers under the newsprint to prevent staining of the surface underneath. Display the mural in this area or in the Community Hall.

CREATION STATION

Theme: The Earth Is the Lord's

Objectives:
- to celebrate God's love as shown in the earth around us
- to learn to care for and appreciate all creation

Bible verse: Lord, you have made so many things! How wisely you made them all! The earth is filled with your creatures. Psalm 104:24 TEV

Setup: Prepare a large poster to identify this as the Creation Station. Create another poster announcing the theme for this area. Plan a garden-like setting to celebrate the beauty of God's world. Use a variety of potted plants, borrowed from church members, or artificial flowers "planted" in pots. Add a pathway (paper grocery sacks cut to resemble stepping stones taped to the floor), bird bath, trellis with vining plants or ribbons on it, water fountain, hammock (or other lawn chair), garden benches, or a pond (a wading pool works well) to your garden. Put picture books and reference books about forests, oceans, caves, and so on, by the hammock so the students can "tour" creation. Include books or pamphlets about conservation of natural resources. A picnic table may be used for the activities in this area. Print the words to the Bible verse on a paper kite to hang in the garden.

Community Activity

Meet a caretaker (All ages).   Invite a resource person to talk to the participants about caring for God's creation. This person could be a farmer, someone from the park service, a librarian who provides age-level appropriate books to read to the students, a person from a recycling plant, and so on. Decide on one project the group can do to care for creation.

Creation Station Activities

Nature wreath (Upper elementary). *Materials needed: corn husks, ribbon, straight pins, foam wreath form, dried flowers or grasses, pinecones, shells, cardboard wreath form.*

If corn husks are being used, gather them and the next three items in the list. If it is not possible to obtain corn husks, a wreath may be made by using the other items listed. Dried grasses may be tied together to form a circle and then decorated, or nature items may be glued to a cardboard wreath form. Be creative!

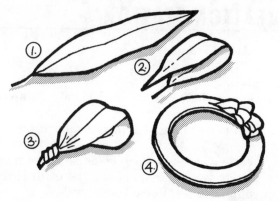

Nature wreath

If corn husks are used, soak them in a bowl of water and remove one husk at a time to work with. Pin each fanned out corn husk onto a foam wreath, using straight pins. As you pin on each husk, overlap the fan portion of the husk to partially cover the one before it. Fill in the wreath form with the husks. A fabric bow may be attached and a wire hanger poked into the back of the wreath.

Thumbprint animal zoo (Lower elementary). *Materials needed: ink pad, typing paper, felt-tip pens or fine-point markers.*

Each participant presses his or her thumb onto a colored ink pad and then onto paper. Use the pens to add legs, tails, ears, and so forth to the thumbprints, and create many kinds of animals. While they are working, talk about caring for pets and other animals. Discuss some endangered species and how we can help preserve God's creatures.

Creation wheels (Preschool). *Materials needed: dinner-sized paper plate, markers, magazines, scissors, glue, paper punch, yarn.*

Read the Genesis creation story to the participants from a Bible story picture book appropriate for the age level. Give each participant a dinner-sized paper plate that has been divided into several parts with a marker. Look through magazines to find pictures of things that God created according to the Genesis account. Cut out and glue the pictures to the various parts of the paper plate. Participants' drawings may be substituted if appropriate pictures cannot be found. Punch holes around the rim of the plate with a paper punch and sew yarn around the plate. Before the session, dip one end of each piece of yarn in glue, shape it into a "needle" and let it dry. Make each piece of yarn long enough to sew all around and have some left for a hanger. Share the story of creation with someone.

Colored salt flower (Preschool, lower elementary). *Materials needed: 8" x 11" lightweight poster board, food coloring, salt, covered containers, glue, pencil, boxes or pans to catch excess salt.*

Make colored salt ahead of time. Put ½ cup salt in a container and add about six drops of food coloring. Cover the container tightly and shake well. Spread the mixture on waxed paper to air dry. Make several colors of salt, including green.

Have the participants sketch a flower with several petals and a stem on the poster board. Talk about the beauty, variety, and delicacy of the flowers God created. Fill in the sketches with salt. Work with one color at a time, only putting glue on the portions of the drawing that will use that color and sprinkling or lightly pouring salt over the glue. Shake off excess salt.

Creation carvings (Elementary). *Materials needed: plaster of paris, vermiculite, water, milk carton, table knife or spoon.*

Mix equal parts of plaster of paris and vermiculite (available in garden shops), and add enough water to make it the consistency of thick cream. Pour it into a milk carton and let it sit until hardened. Make one block per student. When the students are ready to carve the blocks, peel away the carton. This substance can be carved using a table knife or a spoon—a sharp knife is not needed. Make animal carvings and display them in the garden. Ducks can be placed in the pond, birds at the feeder, animals on the lawn, and so on!

Desert in a jar (Upper elementary). *Materials needed: clean glass baby food jars with tight-fitting lids, colored chalk dust, fine sand, heavy paper, stapler, pencils.*

One of the wonderful environments God created is the desert. The sands of deserts in various parts of the world are of different colors. To celebrate this gift of God, make a miniature desert in a jar.

Each participant needs a clean glass baby food jar with a tight-fitting lid. Prepare four colors of sand in plastic buckets by stirring in colored dust created by rubbing colored chalk on a rough surface. Roll and staple heavy paper to make funnels. Pour the colored sand or salt through each funnel into the jar, making each layer a different color. A pencil can be used to poke holes and designs through the layer of sand near the side of the jar before pouring in the next layer. Be sure the jar is completely full of sand. After putting the lid on, remind the participants not to shake the jars or turn them upside down.

HOME COURT

Theme: Love One Another

Objectives:
● to celebrate God's love as revealed in others
● to find ways to share love with each other

Bible verse: Let love make you serve one another. Galatians 5:13b TEV

Setup: Prepare a large poster to identify this as the Home Court. Create another poster announcing the theme for this area. Bring in a rug, rocking chair, lamp, and table, or similar items to represent a family living room. Hang framed pictures on a wall or divider. Print the Bible verse on paper and place the paper in a frame to hang it. The frames may be made of construction paper or cardboard. Pillows and a quilt will add a homey atmosphere.

Community Activity

Reaching out (All ages). Involve the participants in an activity that demonstrates loving and serving others. Collect items to send to a world relief agency, such as health kits—soap, toothbrushes, and so on. Or make paper baskets filled with simple treats or a cheery note with a Bible verse to take to a children's hospital, a care facility, or a family that has a new baby. Select one activity that will work well for your particular situation. If possible, personally deliver cards and baskets as a group activity.

Home Court Activities

Heart bookmark (Upper elementary). *Materials needed: pattern of 1" and 2" hearts, 1" x 11" red ribbon, pinking shears, red and white felt, glue, black permanent marker.*

Make a 1" heart and a 2" heart for the participants to use as patterns. Give each person a piece of red ribbon 1" wide by 11" long. Have the participants use pinking shears to cut four hearts from red or white felt. They should each cut two small hearts and two large hearts using the patterns. Have them glue the top of the ribbon between the two small hearts and the bottom of the ribbon between the two large hearts. Then, using a black permanent marker, they can carefully print "Love One Another" on the ribbon. Encourage them to give their bookmarks to family members or friends.

Picture toast (Preschool). *Materials needed: bread, food coloring, milk, margarine tubs or similar containers, small pastry brushes, toaster.*

Make various colors of edible paint by mixing a drop of food coloring into a small amount of milk. Have several colors in small margarine tubs or similar containers. Have two or more small pastry brushes for each color. Keep the brushes in only one color. Do not move them from one color to another. Paint faces or designs on slices of untoasted white bread. (*Too much paint on the bread will cause it to be soggy, not toast well, and taste awful.*) Toast the bread, show the results to the group, and then eat and enjoy! Before you eat, be sure to pray together, thanking God for the food.

Love place mats (Preschool, lower elementary). *Materials needed: construction paper, pieces of sponge, scissors, tempera or acrylic paints, crayons or markers, clear self-adhesive paper.*

Family members can be reminded of their love for each other by having "I Love You" place mats decorating their places at the table.

Cut sponges in the shape of hearts. Put paint in a shallow container. Distribute construction paper and have each participant print "I Love You" across the center of the paper. They may wish to personalize the place mats by adding a family member's name to each one. Have adult assistants do this for preschool children. Dip the heart-shaped sponges lightly into the paint and make prints around the border of the construction paper. When the paint is dry, have adults apply clear self-adhesive paper to the front and back of the place mats to make them durable and washable.

Family totem poles (Preschool, lower elementary). *Materials needed: paper towel tube, paints, construction paper, magazine pictures, fabric scraps, buttons, glue, cardboard.*

For each participant, divide a paper towel tube into sections to make one section for each member of that person's family. (If someone has a large family, two

Family totem pole

tubes may be needed.) Using paints, construction paper, magazine pictures, fabric scraps, and buttons, design totem poles. Each section of a totem could include a drawing of one family member, his or her hobbies, interests, job, favorite things, favorite color, or other appropriate symbols. When complete, make tabs to glue the pole on a cardboard base so it will stand. Ask participants to talk about the people on their family totem poles, giving them an opportunity to know one another better.

Mystery messages (Upper elementary). *Materials needed: 9" x 12" sheet of construction paper, eight 1" x 12" strips of construction paper, ruler, scissors.*

Provide each participant with a 9" x 12" sheet of construction paper and eight 1" x 12" strips of construction paper in a contrasting color. Fold the large sheet in half lengthwise. With a ruler, mark the sheet in 1" segments. Cut each mark from the fold side to within ½" from the other edge, then unfold the paper. Use the eight strips to weave through the sheet. Create a message by printing one letter in each square across the mat. Print letters on both the strips of the mat and the woven strips. The message may be a favorite Bible verse, or "God Loves You and So Do I" or some similar message.

To make a "mystery message" puzzle, turn the mat over and number the strips from 1–8, beginning at the top. Remove the strips from the mat. Give the puzzle to someone else and challenge that person to weave the strips into the mat to discover the message.

Mystery message

"Helping People" puppets (Preschool, lower elementary). *Materials needed: scissors, construction paper, felt-tip markers, glue, yarn, tape.*

Ask the participants to make puppets to represent people who share God's love with them by helping them. For each person, cut a rectangle of construction paper 3" wide and as high as his or her index finger. Decorate the center of the rectangle with a face, clothes, a hat, and so forth. They can make features with felt-tip markers, and by gluing pieces of yarn to their puppets. Roll the paper into a cylinder that fits loosely on the finger, and glue or tape it together. Invite the group to put on a simple play using their puppets and describing how the people act as helpers.

Strings of fruit (Lower elementary). *Materials needed: patterns of fruit shapes, scissors, colored felt, needle and embroidery thread, mixture of allspice, whole cloves, and broken bits of cinnamon sticks, glue, yarn.*

Jesus says that when we love God, we show it through our loving words and actions. Jesus calls our love and loving actions "fruit." He wants us to show our thankfulness to God by loving others and becoming "fruit producers."

Make patterns of fruit shapes. Cut out the shapes and trace around them on felt: red for the apple, yellow for the banana, and so on. Cut out two pieces of felt for each fruit being made. Each participant should make every kind of fruit.

Thread each needle with several strands of embroidery thread in colors that complement the felt. Stitch together the two sections of each fruit, using an overhand stitch, similar to the method used in lacing. Leave a small opening at the top and put in a mixture of the spices before the last stitches are made. Cut leaves of green felt and glue them to the top of the fruit.

Braid together 24" lengths of yarn. Make a loop at the top for hanging, and then space the four fruits along the yarn. Glue or sew the fruits in place on the yarn braid.

PRAISE PLACE

Theme: Do Everything in the Name of the Lord Jesus

Objectives:
- to celebrate God's love in our worship
- to learn how to worship God at all times

Bible verse: Whatever you do, work at it with all your heart, as though you were working for the Lord and not for [people]. Colossians 3:23 TEV

Setup: Prepare a large poster to identify this as the Praise Place. Create another poster announcing the theme for this area. Paint a large backdrop to resemble the altar area of a church. Set up a table with a Bible, a cross, and candles. Use paraments, if you like. If practical, place several chairs together to look like pews. Hang words and symbols of worship from the ceiling, along with balloons, banners, and other festive items. Print the Bible verse on fabric with fabric paints and hang as a banner.

Community Activity

Stained-glass window (All ages). *Materials needed: typing paper, newspaper, thick black permanent marker, salad oil, crayons, stapler or duct tape.*

Give each participant a sheet of typing paper. Cover the work area with layers of newspaper. Each person will create one pane of a large stained-glass window for the Praise Place, so the group may wish to plan how it will look when all the panes are put together.

On the typing paper, have each participant use a thick, black permanent marker to outline a simple picture or symbol, creating a leaded-glass effect. Draw a black frame around each sheet with the marker. Pour a little salad oil on each picture and spread it out with a paper towel. Color the picture with crayons, pressing heavily on the oil-coated paper. When dry, staple or use duct tape to hold the window sections together and create a large stained-glass window. Hang it in the Praise Place. For the best effect, place a light source behind the paper or hang it in front of a window.

Praise Place Activities

Praise processional and recessional (All ages). Make sure everyone has something to carry—balloons, banners, crepe paper streamers, musical instruments. Begin by reading Psalm 100 or 150. Have participants who play musical instruments practice a song that speaks about love. The song should have a four-beat measure. Explain to the others that they can march to the four beats in the song.

Move into the church sanctuary. Have the group sing, play instruments, and march toward the altar. If possible, ask the pastor to join the processional and then explain various items in the church sanctuary and how they are used in worship. Make sure there is an opportunity to hear the organ, see the place where communion ware and the pastor's robes are kept, and hold the processional cross or large altar Bible. Talk about the parts of the worship service and help everyone to see that worship is a beginning place for our worship out in the world. Worshiping together helps God's people prepare for worshiping in their jobs, their homes, at school, on the playground, and in their neighborhoods. Again sing, play instruments, and march out to participate in the recessional.

Coffee-filter designs (Preschool). *Materials needed: newspaper, dropper bottles of food coloring, wet coffee filter, white construction paper, glue.*

Cover the work area with newspaper. Use dropper bottles of food coloring to drip different colors onto a wet coffee filter. Allow it to dry, then mount it with glue on white construction paper. The colors remind us of the beautiful stained glass we see in some churches.

Praise pockets (Preschool, lower elementary). *Materials needed: 12" x 18" sheet of construction paper, markers, cardboard shirt pocket patterns, glue, magazine pictures, 3" x 5" index cards.*

Give each participant a 12" x 18" sheet of construction paper. The title "Praise Pockets" may be printed on top with markers. Create several 4" x 5" shirt pocket patterns from cardboard. Use the patterns to cut, or let the children cut, four pockets per child from construction paper in a variety of colors.

Label the pockets with categories of things for which we praise God—friends and families, people who share God's love, food, animals, flowers, the weather, and so on. Glue the pockets to the large sheet of construction paper. Cut pictures from magazines of items that fit the categories chosen. Let the participants choose from the collection of pictures, glue their choices on index cards, and put them in the pockets.

Praise pockets

Suggest that the participants keep these near the dining table in their homes and use the pictures as prayer starters. Each family member can draw a picture from a pocket and say a prayer of thanks and praise for that item.

"Thank You, God" shirts (Elementary, upper elementary). *Materials needed: plain T-shirts, fabric paints, cardboard; stencils, sponges (optional).*

Have each participant bring a plain T-shirt. Discuss some of the things for which the children are thankful. Encourage them to create a design for the T-shirt that would say "Thank You, God" and incorporate words or pictures of some of the things identified in the discussion. You may wish to have them do a sketch on paper before starting on the shirts. Have large pieces of cardboard inside the T-shirts during painting to prevent the paint from bleeding through to the back of the shirt. Additional design ideas can be provided by having stencils of hearts, flowers, animals, rainbows, or other shapes. To use these, lay them on the T-shirt and dab the area with a piece of sponge that has been dipped in fabric paint.

Prayer plaque (Upper elementary). *Materials needed: assorted pieces of wood, sandpaper, stain, soft drink can tabs, small nails, hammer, picture cards (religious, Christmas), matches, glue, decoupage paste, brush or sponge, typing paper, pen.*

Prayer is a very important part of every Christian's life. Talking to God in prayer is not just for church time, but for every day as we meet the opportunities, challenges, and problems in life.

Sand the edges of assorted pieces of wood. Stain and let them dry. Nail a soft drink can tab to the back as a hanger. Provide a variety of picture cards, such as religious or Christmas ones. Have the participants copy the words of a favorite Bible verse on paper. Carefully burn or tear the edges of the messages and the pictures selected by the students. Have the students glue their selections to the wood, centering them so that the wood serves as a frame. Pour a small amount of decoupage paste onto the center of the picture and carefully spread it out with a brush or sponge. Cover the top completely, then let it dry. A second coat may be applied, if desired.

Popcorn cake (All ages). *Materials needed: popcorn, 24-oz. package of miniature marshmallows, margarine, gumdrops or plain M & M's, angel food cake pan.*

Pop 8 quarts of hull-less popcorn. Melt a 24-ounce package of miniature marshmallows in a stick of melted margarine. Combine the popcorn with a 10-ounce package of small gumdrops or plain M&M's. Add the marshmallow mixture to the popcorn mixture and mix well. Press into a greased angel food cake pan. Set until firm. Break apart and enjoy.

Metal punch ornaments (Upper elementary). *Materials needed: metal lids from frozen juice cans, cardboard symbol patterns, typing paper, pencils, scissors, tape, medium-sized nails, hammers, scraps of wood, a large nail, yarn or ribbon.*

Develop familiarity with the symbols of the church by featuring them on decorative ornaments. Make cardboard patterns of several symbols, such as various kinds of crosses, a star, a dove, symbols for the Trinity, or a rainbow. Have the participants trace a symbol onto typing paper. Center the symbol that has been traced over a juice can lid and sketch around the lid. Cut off the extra paper and tape the pattern to the lid in several places around the edge. Place each lid on a piece of scrap wood on the floor. Use a medium-sized nail and a hammer to make a series of punches at intervals along the outline of the design. Remove the paper pattern and use the large nail to make a hole near the top. Tie a piece of yarn or ribbon through the hole for a hanger.

Metal punch ornaments

Cardboard-tube trumpets (Preschool). *Materials needed: paper towel tube, rubber band, 4" square of waxed paper, construction paper, glue, markers, blunt needle..*

Make these instruments for the participants to use in worship. Give each one a paper towel tube, a rubber band, and a 4" square of waxed paper. Cut construction paper to fit around the cardboard tube and tape or glue it to the tube. The participants can decorate the tubes using markers. Use a blunt needle to punch a hole about 1" from the end of each tube. Secure the waxed paper over the end of the tube using a rubber band. Participants can hum into the open ends of their tubes to play the instruments.

WORLD VIEW

Theme: Go Therefore and Make Disciples of All Nations

Objectives:
- to celebrate God's love by sharing it with others
- to discover how others have shared God's message of love

Bible verse: How wonderful is the coming of messengers who bring good news! Romans 10:15b TEV

Setup: Prepare a large poster to identify this as the World View activity area. Create another poster announcing the theme for this area. Display a large world map. If possible, mark with pins the places where your local congregation or national church group supports a ministry. Use dividers or a wall to display mission materials, pictures, and other materials showing people sharing the gospel of God's love. Print the words to the Bible verse on an inexpensive map of your town, country, state, or province and place this on display.

Community Activity

Human family collage. (All ages). God's love is for everyone. Read Matthew 28:19 to the students. What does Jesus ask us to do? (*Make disciples of the whole world!*) Pull out pages or cut pictures from travel magazines, travel brochures, and other periodicals that show people who represent all races and cultures of God's people. Glue them collage-style to a large sheet of paper. Title it "God's Love Is for Sharing" and mount it in the World View area.

World View Activities

Our missionaries (All ages). Do some research on missionaries whose work is supported by your congregation or denomination. Gather pictures of them and of their work. Share stories of their experiences in bringing the message of God's love to the people to whom they minister.

Tie-dye from India (Upper elementary). *Materials needed: 12" x 18" pieces of white fabric, two bright fabric dyes, paint shirts, old broom handle, rubber bands, rubber gloves, paper towels, iron, needle and thread, dowel.*

Cut lightweight white fabric, such as old sheets, into 12" x 18" pieces. Prepare two bright fabric dyes in separate containers. Have the participants wear paint shirts. Fold the fabric in half lengthwise. Gather it together like an umbrella around an old broom han-

dle or other stick. Hold the fabric in place with rubber bands at different points and in different patterns along the entire length of the fabric on the stick. The participants may choose either dye, or use both colors if they wish. Immerse the fabric in dye and leave it there as long as the package directions suggest. Squeeze out excess dye, wearing rubber gloves if you wish. Remove the rubber bands and put them on again in a new pattern if you are using a second color. Squeeze out excess dye. Blot with paper towels. Roll the rubber bands off the end of the stick, let the fabric dry, and then iron. Sew a hem across the top of the banner with a long running stitch and insert a dowel or stick for hanging.

Tell participants that this tie-dye method comes from India. Help them locate India on a map and discuss missionaries and others who spread the good news there.

Flower lei from Polynesia (Preschool). *Materials needed: foam egg carton (white and colored), scissors, markers, knitting needle, bobby pins, plastic straws, yarn, construction paper or tissue paper.*

In the Polynesian islands, a flower necklace, or lei, is offered as a welcome and a sign of friendship. Provide one foam egg carton per participant. Cut the egg cups apart and trim. Draw flower petals on the outside of the cups with markers and cut accordingly. With the knitting needle, punch a hole in the center of each cup. Cut plastic straws into 2" pieces. Tie a 36" length of yarn to a bobby pin, which will be used as a needle. String the cups and plastic straws alternately onto the yarn. Make paper flowers by adding construction or tissue paper cutouts to the strand.

Lei

Piñata from Mexico (Preschool). *Materials needed: paper grocery bag, bright-colored crepe paper streamers, scissors, glue, transparent tape, construction paper, wrapped candy treats or snacks, heavy string or twine, stick or broom handle.*

A favorite part of a celebration in Mexico is the piñata. Made of papier-mâché, the piñata is filled with gifts and candy. The children are blindfolded and given a stick with which they try to break the piñata.

Have the participants help decorate a paper grocery bag as a substitute for a papier-mâché piñata. Crepe paper streamers and shapes cut from construction paper may be taped or glued to the bag. Put the candy or snacks into the bag, tie it shut, and suspend the bag from the ceiling or a wide door frame.

Participants can take turns being blindfolded and trying to break open the bag, using a stick such as a broom handle. Monitor the activity carefully so no one gets hit with the stick. Share the contents when the bag is broken.

Batik eggs from Java (Upper elementary). *Materials needed: hard-boiled eggs, sharpened white crayon, egg dye or food coloring, paper towels.*

On the island of Java in Indonesia, people create designs on fabric with wax and dyes. Use hard-boiled eggs to experiment with the batik method. With a sharpened white crayon, carefully draw a design on the egg. Mix egg dye or food coloring in a cup. Dip the egg in the solution until a strong color is present. Remove the egg with a spoon and place it on a paper towel to dry.

Hebrew dreidels (Elementary). *Materials needed: copies of dreidel pattern, scissors, transparent tape, pencils, crayons or markers, raisins, nuts, or some other treat.*

Review the story of Queen Esther in the Bible or consider reading a condensed version of the story to the participants from a Bible storybook. In remembrance of how she saved their ancestors in Persia, the Hebrew people celebrate a special holiday called Purim. One of the holiday games is played with a dreidel (DRAY-dul).

Draw an enlarged version of the pattern shown here. Each square should be 2½″ and the tabs ⅜″. Make copies of your pattern for each participant. Have them cut out the shape, write the words as shown here, and decorate the squares. Make two holes, in the places indicated, with a pencil. Remove the pencil, assemble the cube with tape, then reinsert the pencil.

Play the game by spinning the dreidel on the point of the pencil. Check the participants for allergies, then give each participant an equal number of peanuts or raisins. Then the participants take turns spinning their

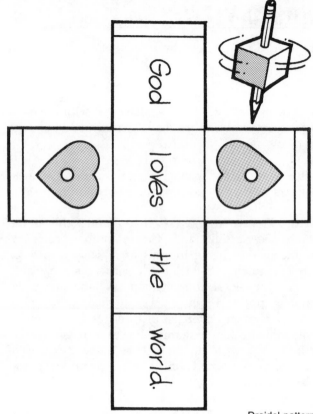

Dreidel pattern

dreidels. Establish the following rules: If the dreidel lands with the word *God* facing up, the person who was spinning will give a raisin or a nut to each of the other players. If it lands with *loves* on top, everyone else gives the spinner a treat. On *the*, the boys in the group give the spinner a treat; on *world*, the girls do. Give each person an opportunity to spin his or her dreidel.

God's love around the world (Elementary and upper elementary). People all over the world need to hear that God loves them. Teach the participants to say "God loves you" in each of these languages.

Spanish: Dios te ama (DEE-ohs tay a-mah)
French: Dieu vous aime (dee-you voo-ZEM)
German: Gott liebt dich (got LEEPT dik)
Japanese: Kami wa anata o aishitemasu (KAH-mee-wah ahna-TAH oh EYE-shtee-mahs)

Practice greeting one another and visitors to the center with these phrases.

Food sampling (All ages). Have a food tasting fair. Bring a variety of foods that people in other countries prepare. Possible foods include tortillas, egg rolls, lefse, fried rice, yams, curried chicken, rice, lima beans, or sugared peanuts.

MISSION EXPEDITION

God's People Continue to Journey with Jesus

The Mission Expedition Center provides the opportunity for participants to explore how Jesus and his followers shared the good news of God's love with others and invited them to join them. It also allows participants to continue on that journey, discovering ways that the Christian church is growing today. The Mission Expedition activities emphasize that the journey with Jesus does not end with the book of Luke. In Acts Jesus' followers are commissioned to pursue the mission of the church throughout the world. Through a variety of learning activities, participants are challenged to find their own roles in the mission of the church.

A central gathering place (Disciples' Dock) and five activity areas (Church Corner, Believers' Village, Promise Shore, Servant Path, and Proclamation Place) provide learning opportunities. Each area includes "Mission Story" activities that focus on how Christians around the world journey with Jesus. Be sure to emphasize that the stories in "Mission Story" are true, but that they represent only one area of a much larger region. Be careful not to generalize about a country and its people on the basis of one story.

Setting up Mission Expedition

The available facilities and the creativity of those involved will determine how Mission Expedition is set up. If possible, use a large area for the complete center, such as a community room, gymnasium, large classroom, or big tent. If one large area is not available, set up in two or three spaces, a separate room for each theme area, or a wide hallway. Consider using outdoor space or making portable theme areas that can be moved from classroom to classroom.

See the description of each activity area for setup suggestions. Mark the walkways among the activity areas by stretching rope or crepe paper streamers between poles set in cans of concrete. Small strips of red fabric may be tied at intervals along the rope. Make the walkways resemble a gangplank by laying down brown shelf paper or craft paper marked to look like boards.

Have guides wear matching sailor hats, boating caps, baseball caps, or newspaper sailor hats to suggest their roles as tour guides.

Prepare a 6" x 9" piece of construction paper, folded to resemble a passport or ticket folder, for each participant and activity area leader or helper. The passport should include the title of this center and the names of the five activity areas on the front cover. On the inside, leave a space for the person's name and

enough room for five 1¼" circles to be placed around the name. Fill an 8½" x 11" sheet of paper with such circles, five in a row. On each set of five circles write the name of a native language and the word for "Jesus" in that language. The languages are those featured in the activity areas. On each set print: Spanish: JESU CRISTO; Pidgin: JISAS; Swahili: YESU; English: JESUS; Japanese: IESU.

When the entire page is full, make enough photocopies of the page so that each participant will receive a set of five circles. Cut the circles apart and distribute the appropriate ones to the activity area where that language will be featured. As participants visit each area, they can glue the appropriate circle to their passports.

DISCIPLES' DOCK

Disciples' Dock is where the participants enter Mission Expedition. This area can be used as:
- a place where activities and schedules are explained;
- a place to share, sing, or tell stories;
- a place to pass out materials or snacks.

Set up this area to look like a boat dock. Construct a bridge-like walkway at the entrance. Write "Disciples' Dock" on a sign hanging over the walkway. Cover the floor with large pieces of corrugated cardboard, drop cloths, or burlap bags.

Post a large world map in the area. Use yarn to circle these locations: Peru, Tanzania, North America, Papua New Guinea, and Japan. Each of these areas is the focus of the mission story in one of the activity areas.

On one side of the area, make a mural from cardboard or plywood to resemble the side of a ship. Cut portholes in the side of the ship. Behind the holes place pictures of how the Christian church is active in mission around the world. Include pictures of your church's programs and projects. Check with your national church magazine or office for global mission for additional pictures. Choose pictures that show growth through service as well as through buildings.

To help the participants realize they are all helping in Jesus' mission today, make a newsprint or brown paper body tracing of each participant. Provide markers or crayons to finish the tracings to resemble travelers or ship workers. Display these drawings around the Disciples' Dock area. Emphasize a different part of the body with each visiting group, and brainstorm with participants ways in which they help the church grow. Ask them to write or draw their own ideas on that body part of their tracing. (*Examples: hands—"I will make cupcakes and bring them to a shut-in"; feet—"I will walk a younger child home from school"; head—"I will think about what I am going to say before I speak"; mouth—"I will greet a new student cheerfully"; heart—"I will be a friend to the new neighbor."*)

CHURCH CORNER

Theme: Journey with Jesus at the Synagogue—Sharing the Good News

Objectives:
- to experience how Jesus commissioned his followers to carry the good news to others
- to discover that the Christian church is built by people

Setup: Make a large poster to identify this as the Church Corner. Create another poster stating the theme for this area. Make part of this area look like a drafting room by placing a drafting table or a bulletin board with actual blueprints by the side of a large rug. Use the blueprints of your own church if they are available or ask for blueprints from a blueprint shop, construction company, or an architect.

Build a sturdy frame for a small church building near the rug or surrounding it. Use cardboard, lumber, lashed branches, or a tent frame. Take care to make sure it is safe for everyone to work with—participants will add items to this frame during several of the activities. You could also use large mural paper or a bulletin board and make a frame from construction paper.

Mission story: North America

Ask the participants to list as many greetings in English as they can. Which do they use most often? Which are from other areas in North America?

A Story to Read Aloud

Several years ago, a group of Christians in Chicago, Illinois, started Bethel New Life, Incorporated, with a special reason in mind. The people at Bethel Church knew they had to do something to save their neighborhood. Many people were moving out because there were not enough clean, safe apartments and houses in which to live. Some people who owned buildings did not take care of them. Soon the buildings

were not safe to live in, so the people living in them had to leave. Then the city would then tear down the unsafe buildings. Almost 200 houses and apartments were being torn down each year.

The members of Bethel New Life each agreed to give five dollars each week until they had saved $5000. They used this money to buy one old house and fix it up. For six months the members worked evenings and weekends repairing the house. When they were finished, they dedicated the building by marching from their church to the house during the Sunday worship service. They were led by the choirs and people carrying crosses.

The neighbors were very surprised by the work the Bethel people had done. It made them want to fix up their own homes. Over 200 people heard about the house that they had fixed and asked if they could live in it. The people at Bethel New Life knew their job was just beginning.

Bethel New Life has worked on hundreds of houses and apartments since that first house. The houses all look cared for, with fences, flowers, and grass. They all have a symbol on them which tells that the people at Bethel were responsible for making them look good again. The people at Bethel feel that each time a house is repaired, it tells the world that God cares for people.

Throughout the years there is one thing that always happens when a project is finally completed. The members of Bethel New Life always dedicate it on Sunday, starting the celebration with morning worship and then marching down the street, carrying balloons and singing gospel songs. This is how they praise God for what they have been able to accomplish.

With the participants, list some ways that the Christians at Bethel New Life are helping others learn of Jesus' love (*providing a safe place to live, helping others improve their houses, parades to praise God, telling people that God cares for them*).

Discuss volunteer efforts in your community that focus on housing rehabilitation.

A Game to Try: Tag

Variations of tag are popular in North America. Try these options as the safe zones or bases: shadows, trees, touching the ground, holding hands with a friend.

A Recipe to Try: Popcorn

Materials needed: popcorn, paper cups, toppings.

Popcorn is a North American treat. Serve it in paper cups and offer a variety of toppings to try: chili powder, seasoned salt, garlic salt, onion powder, grated cheese, or cinnamon and sugar mixture.

Church Corner Activities

The cornerstone (All ages). *Materials needed: paving brick, patio block, or large rock; latex acrylic paint (or mix two parts liquid tempera with one part white glue), paint shirts, cleanup supplies, brushes, newspapers.*

A special stone is often inscribed and set in an important part of the building. If your church building has a cornerstone go look at it. Tell how Jesus is the cornerstone—the most important part—of the church. Give participants a paving brick, patio block, or large rock to remind them of this important truth. Supply paint, paint shirts, cleanup supplies, and brushes. Encourage the participants to design their personal cornerstone with Christian symbols, words, or pictures. Set the completed bricks on newspaper to dry, then place them around the base of the church building frame. At the conclusion of the Mission Expedition Center, they can be used at home as doorstops, paperweights, or bookends.

Frame (Preschool, lower elementary). *Materials needed: craft sticks, glue, markers, ink pad, poster board precut to fit stick frame, yarn, tape.*

Tell how on top of the foundation is the frame that supports the building. The people in our church are like the foundation—each person does what he or she does best, and with everyone working together, they make sure that the things that are needed get done. Ask the students to think of people who help in their church (*janitor, pastor, organist, teachers, secretary, committee member, council member*). Discuss the different gifts and talents these people possess. Point out how each person has something to share.

Frame

Help participants glue four craft sticks together to form picture frames. Paint the frames or color them with markers. Have each participant press her or his finger on an ink pad and make a fingerprint on a piece of poster board precut to fit the craft stick frame. Remind them that their fingerprints are different from all others, just as their ways of helping in the mission of the church show different gifts. Glue the poster board behind the frame, adding a loop of yarn at the top. Use a black marker to write "God's Special Helper" and the participant's name on the frame sticks. Tape or tie the pictures to the church building frame.

Wall of love (Upper elementary). *Materials needed: two 12" x 4" pieces of construction paper in different colors, scissors, tape, yarn or string.*

The mission of the church is held together by people with hearts that trust and love Jesus. Create the walls for your church building frame with Danish heart baskets.

Each basket will use two pieces of construction paper, 12" x 4". Use two different colors. Fold each piece in half so the pieces measure 6" x 4". Holding the two pieces together to make the cuts, round off the top corners of the pieces, as shown. Next, make four cuts of equal width from the folded edges out toward the curved edges.

Hold color 1 at a right angle to color 2. **Remember: The strips are woven through the loops, not over and under the loops.** Weave the top strip of color 1 through the top strip of color 2. Weave the second strip of color 2 through the top strip of color 1. Weave the top strip of color 1 through the third strip of color 2. Weave the fourth strip of color 2 through the top strip of color 1.

Next weave the top strip of color 2 through the second strip of color 1. Weave the second strip of color 1 through the second strip of color 2. Continue weaving strips in this alternating fashion until all strips are woven and a heart-shaped basket is formed. You should actually be able to open the two hearts and have a basket there. An additional strip of paper can be glued on for a handle.

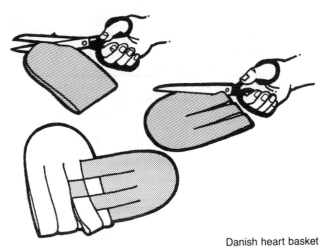

Danish heart basket

Tie several rows of string between the uprights of the church building frame. Use yarn or tape to attach the heart baskets to the rows of string. Space them evenly to help form walls.

Handmade roof (Preschool, lower elementary). *Materials needed: grocery bags, scissors, string, tape.*

Serving hands help build the church. Construct a thatched roof for the building frame by having participants trace their hands onto grocery bags. Cut out the hand tracings and write or draw one way to reach out a hand of friendship to others (*smiling, sharing toys, hugging, helping with a chore*). Tie pieces of string across the top of the church building frame to suggest a roof area. Lay the hand prints on top of the strings to form the roof covering. Secure with tape from underneath.

Mosaic cross-crosslet (Elementary). *Materials needed: Cross patterns, cardboard, scissors, glue, waxed paper or newspaper, small shells, aquarium gravel, squares of tissue paper, confetti, or paper punch dots, clear craft spray.*

A cross is often placed on top of a newly built church as a symbol of our faith in Jesus Christ. To make crosses for the church building frame, make an enlarged version of the cross pattern shown here. It should fit on a sheet of typing paper. Make copies of the pattern for the participants. Glue the paper pattern to lightweight cardboard. Cut out the circle. Working on a piece of waxed paper or newspaper, put a light coat of glue on one small section of the cross at a time, and create a mosaic by arranging small shells, aquarium gravel, squares of tissue paper, confetti, or paper punch dots on the wet glue. When the crosses are dry, you may want to spray them with a clear craft spray. Attach the dry crosses to the top of your church building frame. This ancient form of the cross, called the cross-crosslet, reminds us of the four points of the compass and that the good news is to be shared with people in all places on earth.

Mosaic cross-crosslet

BELIEVERS' VILLAGE

Theme: Journey with Jesus to the City—Responding in Faith

Objectives:
● to learn how Jesus empowered his followers to help others respond in faith to the gospel
● to become aware of the Christian church in Japan

Setup: Make a large poster to identify this as Believers' Village. Create another poster stating the theme for this area. Create a marketplace by making market stalls from large cardboard cartons, card tables, or wood. Drape canopies made from canvas or heavy fabric above the market stalls, keeping fire safety in mind. Leave an open space at the center of the activity area and lay down a piece of canvas or a woven mat. Ask participants to take their shoes off when entering the area, as a visitor to a Japanese home would do. If you have posters or artwork from Japan, they could also be displayed. Place library books about Japan in one of the market stalls. Place materials for the center activities in pots, baskets, and other containers and place them in the stalls, creating learning centers.

Mission Story: Japan

The first time you see someone during the day, say "Ohayo Gozaimasu" (o-hi-o go-zi-ee-mas). This means "Good morning." Between 10 A.M. and 6 P.M., say "Kon Nichiwa" (cone nee-chee-wah). This means "Good day." After 6 P.M. say "Kon Ban Wa" (cone bon wah). This means "Good evening."

A Story to Read Aloud

In Tokyo, a group of 25 Christians joined together to form a church. They met in a garage. For many years no more people joined the small church. They decided to move their church to a part of Tokyo where many families were moving. Ten other churches in Tokyo said they would help move the small church and work to find new Christians to join.

The 10 churches tried to agree on a plan to help the little church. But there were many different opinions. The pastor feared that the church would never be built.

Then an amazing thing happened. The people in the little church found just the perfect piece of land on which to build their new church. The 10 churches in Japan paid two-thirds of the price and churches in North America paid the other third of the money for the land. A congregation was formed before there was even a church building, and grew to 40 members in just one year! These members built a new church building with help from the 10 churches.

The Japanese churches learned a lot about sharing the good news of Jesus' love as they worked together on this project. They plan to work together to start more new churches in areas that do not have any.

God can use the little things we do to accomplish great things. Very few people accomplish great things, but we can each help in little ways in the family, church, and community by praying, studying God's Word, and doing what God has taught us to do. All the little things added up can do great things!

Ask the participants to think of ways people in their church cooperate to do the work that needs to be done.

A Game to Try: Hop

Ten or more players form two teams. Each person has a stick. Each team lays its sticks in a row, like the rungs of a ladder. The sticks are laid 18" apart. The teams line up single file, facing the first stick. When a leader calls, "Go," the first player on each team hops on one foot over each of the sticks, picks up the last one, and hops back. He or she taps the next player, who hops over the remaining sticks, picks up the last one, and hops back again. This continues until one team has picked up all its sticks. Any player who touches a stick with a foot or puts down the second foot must start over.

A Recipe to Try: Egg Flower Soup
   3 cups clear canned chicken broth
   Dash of salt
   Chopped scallion
   1 tablespoon cornstarch
   2 tablespoons water
   1 egg, beaten
   Bring chicken broth to a boil. Separately, add water slowly to the cornstarch and stir. Add cornstarch liquid to the broth. Stir until it begins to thicken and becomes clear. Add salt. Pour the beaten egg into the broth and continue to cook. It will cook quickly. Top with scallion.

Believers' Village Activities

Pentecost story (All ages). Power to continue Jesus' journey comes to us from the gift of the Holy Spirit. Divide the learners into three groups and assign each group a Pentecost sound (*whistling or shaking a pom pom for wind; mumbling or humming noises for the crowd; and sizzling, crackling sounds or rustling paper for the fire*). Tell the story of Pentecost (Acts 2:1-12) with each group making its sound at the appropriate time. End with all three groups making their sounds together and waving red crepe paper streamers. Say that when the Holy Spirit came upon the people, they responded by spreading the good news about Jesus.

Paper lanterns (Elementary). *Materials needed: two 9" x 12" sheets of construction paper of different colors, scissors, tape or glue, yarn.*

These lanterns resemble those used in Japanese communities. Hang them from the ceiling of Believers' Village. Fold a 9" x 12" sheet of construction paper to make a 9" x 6" rectangle. Then make cuts from the fold approximately 5" long and ¾" apart. Open the paper and roll it into a tube (*the slashes will run vertically*). Overlap the edges of the tube and glue or tape. Make another tube from another color of construction paper. Slip this tube into the bottom of the first tube. Slide the top and bottom of the outside tube together, so that the outside tube fans out in the middle. When about 2" of the inner tube shows both above and below the first tube, glue or tape the tubes together. Run yarn through the top for hanging.

Paper lantern

Memory game (All ages). *Materials needed: 10 pair of sanded wood scraps or blocks, markers, small blank cards, glue.*

People who believe in Jesus learn many things from each other. Such learning is an important part of each person's mission expedition. Have older participants make a game of memory match-up for younger participants, using sanded wood scraps or blocks as the playing pieces. To make the pieces, divide a Bible verse, writing the two parts on small cards or cut pairs of identical pictures from old Sunday school curriculum. Glue each pair on two blocks of wood. Make at least 10 pairs. To play, mix the pairs, arrange face down on the floor, and attempt to make matches by taking turns revealing two blocks at a time. If a match is made, the blocks are removed and placed beside the player. If no match is made, the blocks are turned face down again.

Resurrection cross (Upper elementary). *Materials needed: pattern sheets, thick boards, hammers, small nails of uniform size, colored string or crochet thread.*

Jesus was nailed to the cross, but the good news is that he is alive! Respond to the good news of the resurrection by making a string art picture of a cross surrounded by a sunburst.

Make an enlarged version on typing paper of the pattern shown here. Make copies of the pattern for the participants. Tape a copy of the pattern sheet on a thick board. Hammer the nails through the markings on the sheet. Strive to keep the nails at a uniform height, at least ½" above the surface of the board. Carefully tear away the paper pattern and discard.

Outline the cross two or three times with colored string or crochet thread. Choose another color to make the sunburst. Fasten that color to the center nail, then take it out and around each outer nail, returning to the center nail each time, until the sunburst is complete.

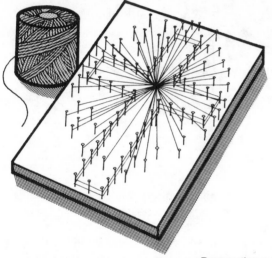

Resurrection cross

Chalk drawings (Preschool). *Materials needed: sugar, water, small pan or plastic container, colored chalk, white construction paper, sponge, paint shirts, cleanup supplies.*

The Day of Pentecost suggests swirls of bright colors as the believers and others gathered for their religious festival. Wet chalk drawings can capture a sense of this day. Add six tablespoons of sugar to 1" of water in a small pan or plastic container. Mix well until the sugar is dissolved. Soak colored chalk in this solution for 10 to 15 minutes to prevent smearing. Have the children put on paint shirts, as chalk stains are difficult to remove from clothing. Dampen sheets of white construction paper with a sponge. Have children draw bright designs (or perhaps crosses, flames, doves, or people) on the damp paper. Help the children clean their hands. Display some of these drawings in the center after they have dried.

Clay crosses (All ages). *Materials needed: clay dough, table knife, cardboard cross pattern, paper clip, oven, clear acrylic spray.*

People around the world who believe in Jesus recognize the cross as a symbol of their faith. Let each participant make a clay cross to hang at home as a reminder of their membership in this worldwide mission of Christians. To make the clay dough, mix ⅔ cup salt, 2¼ cups flour, and ¾ cup water. Add food coloring if desired. Knead the dough until it is smooth. Roll out about ½" thick. Use a table knife to cut out a cross shape. (*You may want to make a cardboard cross pattern to cut around.*) While the clay is still wet, add texture to the cross by pressing designs and textures into the dough with toothpicks, screws, combs, the eraser end of a pencil or other objects. Push a paper clip or loop of wire into the top or back for hanging. Bake the crosses at 250 degrees for about 2½ hours. Crosses can be painted when cool, or sprayed with a clear acrylic finish.

PROMISE SHORE

Theme: Journey with Jesus by the Sea—Trusting in God

Objectives:
● to explore how trust in God empowers our Christian witness and mission
● to learn about Christians in Papua New Guinea

Setup: Make a large poster to identify this as the Promise Shore activity area. Create another poster stating the theme for this area. Hang blue mural paper (or white shelf paper painted blue) in a semicircle around this area. Provide participants with fish shapes cut from sponges and with shallow dishes of tempera paint to create an underwater scene on the mural paper. In front of the mural, place a large tub or children's wading pool half-filled with sand. You might want to put a large sheet of plastic under the pool or tub to catch spilled sand. Place a sprinkling can and small rake nearby to keep the sand smooth and damp for drawing. Provide long sticks for children to use when drawing designs in the sand. If you are able to find travel posters of Papua New Guinea or other South Pacific nations, post those as well. Library books about Papua New Guinea can be placed on a beach towel for a quiet reading area.

Mission Story: Papua New Guinea

"Fele!" (fay-lay). This greeting is from the Begesin people in Papua New Guinea. A *fele* is a woven coconut mat that is placed by the door. When one says "Fele!" it means "Come, you are welcome. The door of my house and of my heart are open to you."

A Story to Read Aloud

Sikorias was a young girl who lived in Papua New Guinea, which is an island in the Pacific Ocean. One day she was attacked by a wild pig in the jungle near her home. Her right arm was very badly hurt by the pig's powerful bite. She was in a lot of pain. Witch doctors wrapped her arm in leaves but by then germs had gotten into the wound and it was infected. She got sicker and sicker. Almost a week later her people carried Sikorias for six hours over the mountains to the missionary they thought might be able to help her.

The missionary could tell that she needed to be in a hospital, but the nearest one was 12 walking hours away, over the mountains and across rivers. Her own people, who had carried her to the missionary, refused to help any further. But the boys who attended the school the missionaries had started had learned about how Jesus loved and cared for the sick. When asked, two teams of four carriers each quickly volunteered to carry the stretcher to the hospital without stopping. Late that night, when Sikorias got to the hospital, the doctors did surgery on her arm. Because the germs had caused an infection that spread to the rest of her body, she was still very, very sick. On the tenth day the fever finally dropped and Sikorias started to get better. Faithful nurses had given her loving care day and night and God had heard the prayers of the new friends she had made at the hospital. Her own family had abandoned her, but her new Christian friends became her family. They took care of her and helped her to grow up as a talented girl and, later on, a Christian women's leader among the people who had saved her life and taught her about Jesus. That's how the Word of the Lord grows in Papua New Guinea and everywhere—one person showing love and telling another person.

Using this story as an example, talk about the many talents and gifts God gives people to help others (*physical strength, medical skills, prayer, teaching, speaking*).

A Game to Try: Conch Shell Bands

Some children who live near the sea in the South Pacific have conch shell bands. Participants can make a similar sound by blowing trumpet-fashion into a cleaned one-gallon plastic jug from which the bottom has been cut. Experiment with the different sounds that can be made with these instruments. Parade around, serenading the other groups with favorite songs.

A Recipe to Try: Sepik (mashed pumpkin and coconut)

For each serving, mix two tablespoons of mashed, cooked pumpkin (canned is fine) with two teaspoons coconut cream (canned is fine). Stir, shape into a ball, and then roll the ball in grated coconut.

If you want to use fresh coconut, make the coconut cream by adding ½ cup hot water to one cup freshly grated coconut meat. Let this stand for 30 minutes, then press the mixture through a sieve. Use additional grated coconut in which to roll the sepik balls.

Promise Shore Activities

Drama (All ages). Read aloud the story of Philip and the Ethiopian from Acts 8:26-40 in the Bible or from a Bible storybook. Discuss how Philip trusted God and went to tell the Ethiopian official about Jesus. Ask volunteers to act out the story as they recall it.

Praise sticks (Preschool). *Materials needed: wooden craft sticks or paint stirrers, several 24" pieces of crepe paper streamers, tape.*

Many Christians express their trust in God through music and motions. To make praise sticks, give a wooden craft stick or paint stirrer and several 24" pieces of crepe paper streamer to each participant. Tape the streamers to the stick. Stand in a circle with each person placing a hand on the shoulder of the person to the right. Hold the praise stick in the other hand. Wave the streamers in a circular motion as you listen to a favorite song and walk in a circle.

Pliers painting (Elementary). *Materials needed: construction paper, small amounts of tempera paint, pie tins, several pairs of pliers, gadgets for printing, such as empty thread spools, large metal nuts (used with bolts), or chunks of sponge.*

A pair of pliers is made of two parts; so is a friendship. Cooperation builds trust between friends. Participants will work in pairs to make two friendship cards to send to others. Provide folded pieces of construction paper and a variety of gadgets that can be gripped by the pliers, dipped in paint and printed on the cards. Place small amounts of tempera paint in pie pans. Give each pair of participants a pair of pliers. Instruct them to work together, each holding one handle of the pliers. Use the pliers to pick up a gadget and proceed as described above. Have each pair complete two cards. When the cards are dry, write a message of friendship on the inside. Plan to give the cards to others.

Treasure hunt (All ages). Jesus' followers responded with trust and obedience to his instructions. Help participants gain experience in following directions by leading them on a treasure hunt in the church buildings or on the church grounds. The treasure hunt can also serve as an opportunity to teach about your church building. You could lead them through the sanctuary, giving clues such as, "Take 10 steps to the right of the pulpit" or "Go to the steps leading up to the altar." Remind the group that the church is God's house and we show respect for God by using good manners there. Have the final clue lead to a "treasure," such as stickers for each participant or a favorite snack.

Giant flowers (Upper elementary). *Materials needed: 12" x 18" sheets of colorful tissue paper, scissors, chenille craft stems.*

Papua New Guinea has many exotic and brightly colored flowers. Brighten up the Promise Shore area with colorful flowers. Let each participant choose four sheets of tissue paper, all the same color or mixed colors. With all four sheets stacked together, accordion fold in folds about 2" wide. Twist a chenille craft stem tightly around the middle of the folded paper. The ends of the folded tissue may be left flat or cut in curved or pointed shapes to form various kinds of flower petals. Separate the layers of tissue (petals) and gently pull each petal up and toward the center of the flower. Continue until all petals are separated. Make adjustments of petals and fluff the completed flower.

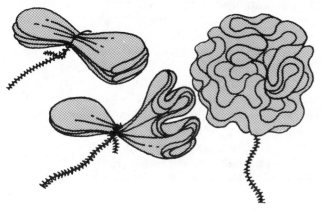

Flower

Paper plate flowers (Preschool). *Materials needed: scissors, paper plates, cotton balls, glue, shallow containers of bright, thick tempera paint, green construction paper.*

Have participants use scissors to cut 1" intervals around the edge of a paper plate. Bend the cut portions in to resemble flower petals. Put glue in the center of each plate and fill the area with cotton balls. Take other cotton balls and dip them lightly in shallow containers of thick tempera paint in bright colors. Dab the paint onto the cotton balls on the plate. If a variety of paint colors is being used, help the children learn how to keep the colors separate by dipping the cotton balls only in the same color time after time. Cut strips of green construction paper for stems. Staple or glue them on. Dabbing paint on the centers of the flowers makes one think of the pollen that is carried on the bodies of bees when they fly from plant to plant—another example of God's great and good plan for creation.

Rainbow mobiles (Lower elementary). *Materials needed: lightweight cardboard, scissors, markers or crayons, glue, cotton balls, paper punch, yarn.*

Rainbows are mentioned in Genesis 9:12-17 as a sign of God's promise to us. We can trust in that promise. Make rainbow mobiles to hang in the Promise Shore area.

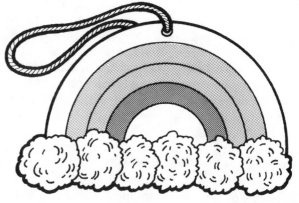

Rainbow mobile

Cut lightweight cardboard into 8" circles. Cut each circle in half. On the half circles, use markers or crayons to draw the color bands of a rainbow. In nature the color order from the outside band is red, orange, yellow, green, blue, indigo, violet. Color both sides of the cardboard. Glue cotton balls along the bottom of the half circle to resemble clouds. Punch a hole in the top of the rainbow and attach a piece of yarn for a hanger.

SERVANT PATH

Theme: Journey with Jesus on the Road—Serving God and Others

Objectives:
- to discover how God gives people power to serve and to be faithful to the mission of the church
- to learn about Christians in Tanzania

Setup: Make a large poster to identify this as the Servant Path. Create another poster stating the theme for this area. Create a long, narrow seating area between two sheets of white mural paper. This area should resemble a road. On the mural paper, designate the following areas, which represent the terrain found in Tanzania and other parts of central Africa. Print the verse from Psalms on a sign for each of the areas: mountains (Psalm 95:4); bush land (Psalm 104:14); jungle (Psalm 96:12b-13a); desert (Psalm 107:35); river and ocean (Psalm 93:4). Ask each group to paint one portion of the mural. Show the participants pictures from an encyclopedia or picture magazine to suggest how to paint the scenes.

If you have posters of Africa or objects such as carvings, baskets, or fabrics, display those as well. Create a quiet reading area by putting a blanket over a table to create a roadside shelter. Place a brightly colored cloth on the shelter floor and put library books about Tanzania and Africa in a basket there.

Mission Story: Tanzania

"Jambo" (jam-boh). This greeting is in Swahili, a language spoken by many people in Tanzania. It means "hello."

A Story to Read Aloud

Yesaya (Yeh-sah-yah) was a man who was a member of the Masai (mah-si) tribe in Africa. He was also a Christian who wanted to share the story of Jesus with his neighbors who had never heard of Jesus. He went to a village called Engudukoiti (en-goo-doo-koh-ee-tee), and lived with the Masai people there for awhile. He told them that God loved them and wanted them to be a part of God's family all over the world. Yesaya taught them Christian songs that they sang to their own Masai melodies and gave them New Testaments, the part of the Bible that tells about Jesus. When it was time for him to leave, Yesaya told the villagers to go to a Christian congregation called Oldonyo Sambu (ohl-dohn-yoh sahm-boo) if they needed help in learning more about being Christians. Oldonyo Sambu was about 10 miles away.

Later, three young people from Engudukoiti went to see some of the church members at Oldonyo Sambu. They opened their New Testaments and said, "We read in this New Testament, but we do not understand it. We read the word *ubatizo* (baptism) and the word *kanisa* (church) but we don't know the meaning. Come and help us!"

So the people in the Oldonyo Sambu congregation sent someone to Engudukoiti every Thursday and every Sunday to teach and to lead them in worship. They worshiped under a beautiful thorn tree. They outlined the place where they worshiped with rocks, with an opening for the door, and this was their church.

The wind and the dust and the rain sometimes made worship in this outdoor church difficult. Eventually the two churches worked together to build a church building. The men cut small trees and used them for walls. Women and children then helped to fill the inside of the walls with rocks before both sides were plastered with mud. The people took an offering to buy corrugated iron for the roof.

But the church building itself is not the most important part of God's work. The best part of the story is that 25 adults and many children at that church were baptized and are now a part of the worldwide Christian family.

How can we tell other people about Jesus? Share some ideas with each other.

A Game to Try: Left/Right

Players form a circle with a leader in the center. All jump and clap in rhythm. The leader jumps in front of one player, and after several jumps calls out either "left" or "right," at the same time extending the left or right foot. The other player must respond by extending the same foot. If able to do it correctly, the player can stay in the circle; if unable, the player becomes "It" and the leader joins the circle.

A Recipe to Try: Sugared Peanuts

Put in heavy pot:

4 cups raw peanuts
1 cup sugar
½ cup water

Boil mixture until water is boiled away. Stir almost constantly to avoid scorching. Spread on a flat pan to cool. Break into clusters or separate into individual sugar coated peanuts.

Servant Path Activities

Serving together montage (All ages). *Materials needed: large cardboard church shape, construction paper, pencils, markers, scissors, tape.*

On our mission expedition, it is important to help each other. Post a large cardboard church shape. Have construction paper and pencils available. Have each participant trace his or her hand on construction paper and write his or her name on the hand tracing. For those old enough to do so, ask them to also write on the tracing something they do to help the church. Younger participants can dictate their responses for adults to record. This may include attending worship and Sunday school, praying, singing in a choir, and so on. Cut out and tape all the hand tracing onto the church shape. When the learning activities have ended, either display the church shape in a prominent place for the whole congregation to see as a reminder of their call to serve the neighbor, or return the individual hand tracings to their owners so that everyone is reminded that he or she is part of the church.

Helping hand plaque (Preschool, lower elementary). *Materials needed: plaster of paris, pie pans or flat boxes, aluminum foil, paper clip, marker.*

Make these plaques to remind participants that they can serve God now and throughout their lives by helping others. Mix plaster of paris and pour it into pie pans or flat boxes lined with aluminum foil. (Make several small batches rather than one large batch, as the plaster hardens very quickly.) Have each person press one hand into his or her plaster form to make a hand print. As the plaster is drying, stick a paper clip that has been bent open into the plaster to make a hanger. When the plaster is dry, remove from the tin and use a marker to write "(*participant's name*) is God's Helper" on the plaque. Do not dispose of excess liquid plaster in a drain; let it harden and then throw it in the trash.

Planter (Elementary, upper elementary). *Materials needed: plastic bottoms from two-liter soft drink bottles, plastic lids, hot water, small stones or gravel, potting soil, several spoons, flower seeds or flowering seedlings; acrylic paints and paintbrushes (optional).*

Flowers help to make the world a more beautiful place and to bring cheer into people's lives. Have the participants make planters that can be given to persons who are homebound or are residents of a care facility.

Remove the plastic bottoms from two-liter soft drink bottles by soaking them in hot water. Place a 1" layer of small stones or gravel in the bottom of the container for drainage. Fill with potting soil and flower seeds or flowering seedlings. Place the planter on a plastic lid, such a margarine tub cover. If you wish, the planters could be decorated with designs or messages done with acrylic paints before the planting begins.

Peanut relay (All ages). *Materials needed: several brooms, peanuts in the shell.*

Peanuts are grown and eaten in Tanzania and other parts of Africa. Use peanuts in the shell for this game. Divide into two teams. Provide each team with a broom. Have each team line up opposite a pile of peanuts. On the starting signal, direct the first person on each team to run to the other end of the room and sweep one peanut back to the end of his or her line. Continue this procedure until each person in the group has had a turn. After all players have returned, provide clean peanuts, not used in the relay, for them to eat. Put the peanuts used in the game outside for animals to eat.

PROCLAMATION PLACE

Theme: Journey with Jesus in the Country—Witnessing in New Places

Objectives:
- to celebrate the progress that has been made in building the Christian church and to dedicate ourselves to continuing the mission
- to learn about Christians in Peru

Setup: Make a large poster to identify this as the Proclamation Place. Create another poster stating the theme for this area. As a backdrop for this center, make a "wall" of red-brown construction paper or paint with that color on a large sheet of paper. Use black marker to draw "bricks." A large drawing of a llama would add atmosphere. Drape white bed sheets or several yards of white fabric across the ceiling to suggest the billowy clouds high in the Andes mountains of Peru. If you have access to posters of Peru or other South American countries, display them—as well as ceramic pots, woven mats or blankets, straw baskets, piñatas, or large plants. Create a quiet reading area in a hammock. Provide library books about Peru and other South American countries.

Mission Story: Peru

"Saludo" (sah-loo-doh). In Spanish this means "hello." "Buenos dias" (bwen-ohs dee-ahs). This means "good day" in Spanish.

A Story to Read Aloud

Bernardo is eight years old. He lives high in the mountains of Peru, in South America. Bernardo is excited because his village has chosen this day for a *faena*, a day when all the villagers come together to work on one project. Today they are building a new house for Bernardo, his mother, and his three younger sisters. His father died last year, and now the family's three-room house needs to be replaced. The heavy rains that last for months in Peru have made the mud bricks of his old house very weak.

As Bernardo watches the men carry the heavy mud bricks and put them into place for walls, he remembers the day last month when he got to walk through the huge mud puddle where his mother was helping mix the pieces of cut straw into the mud to make a cement-like mixture. They called that work the "mud dance." The mud mixture was then poured into brick molds and left to harden in the sun.

Bernardo's mother is also excited about the new house. She has promised the small group that meets for Bible study in their village that the next meeting could be in her house. They gather in people's homes for Bible study because the church needs many repairs and it takes too many candles to make it light enough for study.

Bernardo has even tried to read some words from the new Bible the missionaries brought to the village. It is difficult because he is just learning to read, but also exciting because the Bible is in the language of his people, the Quechua (keh-CHOO-wa) language. Bernardo remembers listening to the adults gathered to read the Bible. They read about a woman named Lydia. She, too, had invited people into her home to learn about Jesus. Bernardo wonders if their new home might become like a little church where neighbors study and worship. Bernardo feels that this is what a church should be.

After telling this story, discuss the many different types of places where Christians can gather to worship and study.

A Game to Try: El Lobo (the Wolf)

Gather in a circle with one participant in the center. Hold hands and circle around the "wolf," chanting, "Playing in the forest, we see a wolf nearby. Wolf, what are you doing?" The "wolf" responds by describing some actions, such as sleeping, eating, going to school, and so on. When the wolf responds, "I'm coming to capture you!" the players in the circle scatter and the wolf chases them until one player is tagged. The one tagged then becomes the "wolf" in the center of the circle.

A Recipe to Try: Alfajores

These cookies are a special treat for children in Peru. For each serving, prepare two simple, flat sugar cookies. Set out a bowl of thick caramel sauce, a bowl of powdered sugar, and a plate of grated coconut. Let participants put caramel sauce between the cookies, sprinkle it with powdered sugar, then roll the edges in coconut.

If you have trouble locating a thick caramel sauce, try mixing the sauce with marshmallow cream to thicken it.

Proclamation Place Activities

Mission expedition (All ages). Invite a missionary to come and speak to the participants about the work that is done in this part of the world. The global mission office of your denomination would be a resource for more information.

Paper mola (Elementary). *Materials needed: bright-colored construction paper, black construction paper, scissors, table salt, colored chalk dust, glue.*

A mola is a colorfully stitched cloth panel popular in South America. The design normally includes symbols in bright colors that are separated from one another by narrow black borders. South America is home to many varieties of colorful butterflies. Cut several paper butterflies in various shapes and sizes. Glue the paper cutouts close together on a sheet of black construction paper. Make colored table salt by mixing salt and colored chalk dust. Make several colors. Put a thin coat of glue on portions of the white butterflies. Sprinkle the colored salt on the glue, keeping in mind that the designs on one butterfly wing are exactly the same on the other—another of God's amazing details. When the glue is dry, shake off the excess salt. Repeat this process, using many different colors. As the participants work, talk about the symbolism of the butterfly in relation to the resurrection.

Church cheers (Preschool, lower elementary). Make up several rousing cheers to proclaim the news about your church. Let the children create the cheering motions. Perhaps an older participant could help with this project. A sample cheer might be:

We're from Calvary,
That's our name!
Won't you come and join us?
You'll never be the same!

Piñata (All ages). *Materials needed: crepe paper, tissue paper, construction paper, brown lunch bags, newspaper, markers, string or yarn, scissors, glue.*

Celebrations in South America are colorful and lively. Celebrate the conclusion of the learning center activities by making colorful decorations to add to the center and to take home. To make bird or fish piñatas, give a paper lunch bag and several sheets of newspaper to each person. Crumple the newspaper and fill the bag two-thirds full. Tie off the top of the bag with yarn or string. Encourage the participants to be creative as they make the bag look like a fish or a bird. Attach string to the top of the piñata and tie to the ropes hanging from the ceiling. Cut out figures, such as birds, butterflies, and flowers to hang in the center as well. At the end, let participants take the piñatas home to fill with candies, toys, or fruit for use at a family celebration.

Weaving (Elementary, upper elementary). *Materials needed: cardboard, thin yarn, ruler, tape, scissors.*

The Quechua (ket-CHOO-ah) people of the Andes mountains in Peru are weavers. For thousands of years they have woven the wool of the llama, alpaca, and vicuna into beautiful cloth.

Try weaving this friendship bracelet.
1. Measure your wrist.
2. Cut a 1½" wide strip of cardboard as long as your wrist measurement, plus 1".
3. On each end of the cardboard cut five ½" deep slits spaced ¼" apart.
4. Cut a 5" piece of yarn and knot one end. Slide the yarn into the first slit and anchor the knot behind the slit. Wind the yarn lengthwise around the cardboard five times, pulling it down into each slit in order. Secure the remaining end with a knot in the back of the last slit. Don't pull the yarn too tightly or the cardboard will bend.
5. Cut a separate 3" length of yarn and wrap a small piece of tape tightly around one cut end to form a "needle." Begin weaving with this "needle" through the five strands of yarn on the front of the cardboard, leaving a 4" tail of yarn. Whenever you want to change colors, cut another piece of yarn. Tie the two colors together, cut the extra ends off, and tuck the knotted ends behind the weaving. Keep the horizontal rows of weaving packed firmly together. When the weaving reaches the bottom of the cardboard, leave a 4" tail of yarn near the knot at the bottom of the cardboard.
6. To finish, slip each knotted end from its slit and tie it to the tail of yarn nearest it. Cut the four strands on the back of the cardboard across the middle and remove the bracelet from the slits. Knot all strands at both ends, close to the weaving. Twist the loose strands together and knot the ends. Fit the bracelet to your wrist and tie it on to wear. Make others to give to your friends.

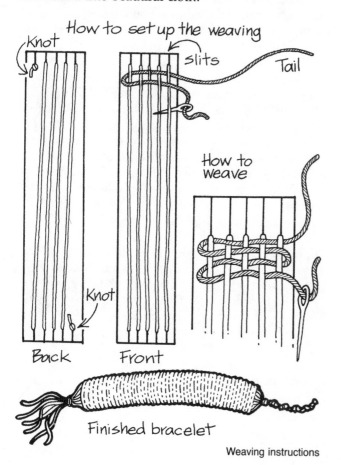

How to set up the weaving
Knot   slits   Tail

How to weave

Back   Front   Knot

Finished bracelet

Weaving instructions

RAINBOW CONNECTION

Rainbow People

What makes us rainbow people? We are precious to God. We stand in awe and wonder at God's majesty and creative powers.

As we find excitement and enjoyment in the beauty and colors of God's creation, the beautiful things we see are often ignored or made the subject of complaints—dandelions ruining the lawn, leaves to rake, snow to shovel.

Rainbow people worship God. They sing joyfully, pray simply, and even clap their hands spontaneously. Rainbow people accept things on faith. They need no fancy theories or explanations; they simply believe and trust. Encountering God on a physical level, they would certainly ask God to join in their play, tell stories to them, and join them on a walk through a field.

We are rainbow people for many reasons. Rainbow people make days brighter, point out the wonders of God, warm the world with smiles and hugs, and encourage everyone in love. When rainbow people worship together, the trust among them strengthens and becomes the hope for the future.

As rainbow people interact with God and with one another through prayer, stories, and worship, they will discover the ability within themselves to grow in faith and reach out in love.

Five Theme Centers

A central meeting place (Promise Gate) and five activity areas (Heritage Hall, Creative Gardens, Exploration Station, Caring Kingdom, and Praise Place) focus on the theme of Christian living.

Setting up Rainbow Connection

Ideally, the Rainbow Connection will be placed in one large area such as a fellowship hall, gymnasium, or large classroom. If this is impossible, use two or three large spaces, or a separate room for each of the five activity areas, and an appropriate and easily visible spot for the Promise Gate.

Display large Rainbow Connection signs and banners at all entrances to the area. Use a variety of rainbows in different sizes to set the tone for the centers. Each activity area will also have an identifying sign or banner. Extra touches such as streamers and hanging symbols will enhance the atmosphere of the center.

The suggestions for each activity area are only starting places. Add your own ideas to reflect the material and people resources available locally.

PROMISE GATE

The Promise Gate will stand at the entrance to the Rainbow Connection. It reminds us of God's promise to love us always. Materials and activities found at the Promise Gate will encourage participants to think about living a Christian life.

Perhaps you can borrow a garden trellis archway to use for the entrance. Cut two large arcs from cardboard and paint them rainbow colors. Cut a slit in the middle of the rainbows (one from the top down and one from the bottom up). Intersect the two pieces and hang the rainbows over the entrance to the Promise Gate.

Make a sign identifying the Promise Gate and hang it from the rainbows. Mount news clippings, photos, and other items related to daily Christian living on brightly colored pieces of construction paper. Hang these on the trellis, a bulletin board, or a nearby wall.

Use the Promise Gate in the following ways:
● as the meeting place where center activities and schedules are explained;
● as a place to share. Have participants collect clippings and items of interest, and add them to the Promise Gate;
● as a place to think. Spending a few minutes at the Promise Gate before entering the Rainbow Connection will give the participants a chance to think about how they are living their Christian lives. Encourage them to spend time discussing their discoveries and insights with one another;
● as a place to gather. "Meet you at the gate." Groups may wish to use the space near the Promise Gate for their story time or as a gathering place for instructions about new activities.

HERITAGE HALL

Theme: Experiencing God's Love

Objectives:
● to become familiar with signs and symbols of our Christian faith
● to explore our heritage as members of the family of God

Setup: Make a large poster to identify this as Heritage Hall. Create another poster stating the theme for this area. Locate Heritage Hall along a wall. Cut stone shapes from gray construction paper and tape them along the bottom of the wall. Write the names of some of God's people, such as Noah, Lydia, and Peter, on other stone shapes and fasten them to the wall.

Leave free space along part of the wall for the Heritage Hall of Fame. Make paper picture frames that the participants can slip pictures into as they make discoveries about God's people. Include a bulletin board to display projects made in the center.

Secure a small bare tree or tree branch in a container of gravel for a symbol tree.

Draw Christian symbols such as a fish, cross, and dove on a poster made of tagboard. Write the name and meaning below each symbol on the chart. Make another set of symbols out of tagboard, and tape these symbols to the floor in a hopscotch format. Check your church library or contact the church staff for reference books containing symbols and their meanings.

Make rainbow armbands for the guides to wear in the center. Write "Heritage Hall" and the guide's name on the armband.

Heritage Hall Activities

Yarn symbols (Preschool, lower elementary). *Materials needed: yarn, church symbols drawn on paper or cardboard with bold marker lines, waxed paper, newspapers, glue, nylon fishing line or thread.*

Make symbol shapes from yarn that has been dipped in liquid starch. Form the shapes on sheets of waxed paper laid over a printed symbol. Let dry. Attach nylon fishing line or thread to the shapes, and hang them from the symbol tree (see "Setup").

Symbol scramble game (All ages). Have the participants sit in a circle on chairs. Have one less chair than the number of players. Assign a different symbol such as a fish, dove, or palm branch to each person. To play, "It" calls the name of two symbols. The participants assigned those symbols exchange places.

Continue doing this for a few times, then "It" calls "Symbol scramble!" At this signal, all participants need to change to a different chair. "It" will now be the person left standing.

Wooden fish stabile (Upper elementary). *Materials needed: 3/8" to 1/2" thick fish shapes cut from a soft kind of wood, newspapers, sandpaper, wood stain, paintbrushes or rags, medium gauge wire, glue, mound of clay.*

Explain that the fish was an early symbol used by members of the Christian church to identify themselves. Enlist an adult volunteer to cut 3"–4" long fish shapes and drill a hole in the bottom of each one to accommodate the wire being used. Also have the wire cut into 4" to 5" pieces by an adult.

Have the participants work on newspaper as they sand the fish and apply wood stain. When dry, poke the piece of wire in the hole and put glue around the wire to secure it. Position the stabile in a 2"–3" mound of clay.

Stuffed symbol shapes (Elementary). *Materials needed: mural paper, scissors, tempera paint and brushes or colored markers, stapler, crumpled newspaper, string.*

Cut two identical symbol shapes from mural paper (examples include fish, cross, shell, and butterfly). Have the participants decorate the symbols with tempera paint or colored markers. When dry, staple the edges of the shapes together, leaving a small section open. Stuff crumpled newspaper into the shape through this opening. Staple shut, then hang the symbols from the ceiling with string.

Butterflies (All ages). Butterflies, the symbol of new life, can be made in a variety of ways. Look for two or three different methods of making butterflies that would be appropriate for the different ability levels of participants coming to the center.

Spatter paint plaques (Elementary, upper elementary). *Materials needed: white paper, clean plastic foam meat trays, 4" x 5" pieces of wire screen, old toothbrushes, tempera paint, glue, newspapers, church symbol shapes made of lightweight cardboard, yarn.*

Cover the entire work area with newspapers. Provide paint shirts to cover the participants' clothing. Cut a piece of white paper to fit the bottom of a foam tray. Arrange cardboard symbols in a pleasing pattern on the paper. Hold a piece of wire screen 9"–10" above the tray and rub an old toothbrush dipped in paint across the screen. This will produce spatters on the white paper. Move the screen from time to time until the paper is covered with the amount of spattering desired. When the paint is dry, remove the shapes. Make two holes through the top edge of the foam tray and tie a piece of yarn through them to form a hanger for the spatter painting.

Heritage Hall of Fame (Elementary, upper elementary). Discuss some of God's people (biblical or contemporary) the participants have learned about in church school or other settings. Give participants a chance to explore the stories and lives of these people. Any Bible story, books, videos, or other resources in your church library will be helpful.

Using what they discover, have them draw portraits of the people they have researched and insert it into a Hall of Fame frame (see "Setup").

Bible "ABCs" (All ages). *Materials needed: 4" x 6" pieces of tagboard in several colors, sandpaper, fabric, fake fur, foil, yarn, ribbon, craft sticks, seeds, glue.*

Make biblical alphabet cards to help teach about people and events in the Bible. Cut 4" x 6" pieces of tagboard (if possible, use several colors). To help young children with tactile learning, cut the letters of the alphabet from sandpaper, fabric, fake fur, and foil. They can also be shaped from scraps of yarn, ribbon, craft sticks, and seeds. After gluing the letters on the cards, participants should spend time brainstorming different names and objects mentioned in the Bible that begin with each letter. Write or illustrate these on the front of the cards.

God's people pantomime (Elementary, upper elementary). Give participants specific Bible references to look up, such as Noah and the ark (Genesis 6–7), Zacchaeus (Luke 19), the good Samaritan (Luke 10), or Jesus' birth (Luke 2). Allow small groups to decide how they will pantomime their story.

Symbol hopscotch (Elementary). Using the tagboard symbols taped on the floor (see "Setup"), let the participants play symbol hopscotch. As they land on a symbol, participants should read about it from the symbol chart. Older participants might read the symbol information if the player cannot read.

CREATIVE GARDENS

Theme: Becoming All I Was Meant to Be

Objectives:
● to give participants the opportunity to use their talents
● to develop an appreciation of God's gift of creativity

Setup: Make a large poster to identify this as Creative Gardens. Create another poster stating the theme for this area. Creative Gardens should be located along a wall. Make letters saying "We Follow Jesus" and attach them to the wall. Arrange an easel or wall space where groups can use chart paper. Designate a "stage" area for use by the rainbow players.

Pot small trees or plants in containers filled with dirt, sand, or gravel. Put these trees and plants in the center for the feeling of a garden. Put a bench near a tree in the garden for a resting place. Attach small artificial birds to the tree branches. Make rainbow armbands for the guides to wear in the center. Write "Creative Gardens" and the guide's name on the armband.

Creative Gardens Activities

"We Follow Jesus" footsteps (All ages). *Materials needed: brightly colored construction paper, tape, chart paper, pen or pencil.*

Trace each participant's foot on brightly colored construction paper. Cut out the prints and have the participants write their names and decorate the footprints as they wish. Tape the footprints on the wall with the words "We Follow Jesus." Put a large sheet of chart paper on the wall beside the footprints. Attach a pen or pencil to the chart with a string. Title the chart "Ways I follow Jesus." Have the participants write the ways they follow Jesus on the chart, or have adults record the responses of younger participants.

Pointillism pictures (Preschool, lower elementary). *Materials needed: cotton-tipped swabs, thick tempera paint, light-colored construction paper.*

Demonstrate a different way of painting, called pointillism, which uses dots of color rather than strokes. Encourage preschoolers to experiment with the method by applying dots in a free-form style. Ask older participants to think of a picture or design that they would like to make. Lightly sketch the design on the paper. Then use the swabs to fill in the spaces in the design with "dots" rather than making strokes with the paint. Looking at the drawing from a distance, the dots will blend together to form the picture. Hang some of the finished art in the center.

Pointillism picture

Friendship rainbows (Upper elementary). *Materials needed: 8" x 10" pieces of burlap, yarn, tapestry needles, 6" x 8" piece of cardboard, yarn, tape, fine-tip marker (optional).*

Make an example of the stitchery banner shown here. Give each of the participants a piece of burlap (or other even-weave fabric), and yarn with which to work. Show them the satin, chain, and french knot stitches to use on their project. The lettering can be done in chain stitch or written with a fine-tip marker when the rest of the picture is completed.

Mount the completed picture by wrapping the edges around the cardboard and taping them to the back. Attach a length of twisted or decorative yarn for a hanger.

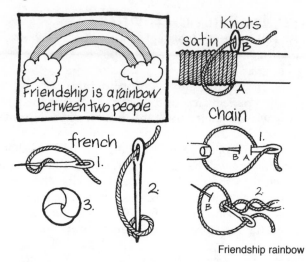

Friendship rainbow

Imagination station (Elementary). *Materials needed: whole sheets and scraps of construction paper, tissue paper, gift wrapping paper, pieces of aluminum foil, buttons, sequins, fabric scraps, needles and thread, glue, and odds and ends of other art material.*

Lay out a wide variety of art materials, such as those listed above, or others that are available. Encourage the participants to choose the materials they find interesting and "create" something from them. Suggest that it can be flat or three-dimensional. Encourage participants to explain what they see and hope to express through their creations.

The rainbow players (All ages). *Materials needed: freestanding cardboard, simple props, Bible.*

Plan several mini-dramas to dramatize living in God's love. Bible stories such as the good Samaritan (Luke 10) and the lost sheep (Luke 15) are possible subjects for dramas. Look in Bible storybooks for other possible stories to enact.

Paint a mural background on cardboard that is freestanding, and make or find simple props. Have participants rehearse and present the dramas in the Creative Gardens "stage" area.

Encourage the participants to recreate situations they might encounter in their own lives. Have them keep the dialog and actions informal.

God's participant book (All ages). *Materials needed: paper punch, white construction paper, pencils, pens, markers or crayons.*

Punch two holes along the edge of sheets of white construction paper. Have each participant write the sentence, "I am God's child. God _____" on one of the sheets of paper. Have them finish the sentence by telling a talent or gift God has given them and then have them illustrate it. Keep adding the pages the participants finish to a book. Make a cover that has the title, "God's Children" on the front. Keep this book in the Creative Gardens area for everyone to read.

Talent show (All ages). Arrange beforehand to have children and adults from the congregation or community visit the center and demonstrate their special talents. This might include musicians, dancers, gymnasts, artists, and other talented people.

Decoupage cans (Upper elementary). *Materials needed: clean, dry cans, enamel paint, seed packet labels or small magazine pictures, rubber cement, white glue.*

Paint the cans with enamel paint. When dry, attach seed packet labels or small magazine pictures to the can with rubber cement. After the glue dries, brush two or three coats of a mixture of half water and half white glue over the entire can. Use the decorated can for holding pencils or a plant.

EXPLORATION STATION

Theme: Loving Relationships with People

Objectives:
● to provide interaction among participants
● to give participants an opportunity to explore their relationships with God and others

Setup: Make a large poster to identify this as the Exploration Station. Create another poster stating the theme for this area. Lengths of brightly colored cloth or paper can be draped from the ceiling to make a tent-like roof.

Create a life-size stuffed mannequin by filling a set of children's clothing with newspaper or other material. Make the head and face from a nylon stocking stuffed with plain cloth. Cut facial features from fabric and glue onto the stocking. A hat can eliminate the need for hair or yarn can be used to make hair, if you wish. Set the stuffed figure in a chair near the entrance to the area, holding a sign that says, "Welcome, friends!"

Make rainbow armbands for the guides to wear in the center. Write "Exploration Station" and the guide's name on the armband.

A rolling cart with cooking utensils and ingredients, situated near an oven, will complete this center.

Exploration Station Activities

Rainbow collage (All ages). *Materials needed: large sheet of paper, photographs of the participants, instant-developing camera and film, letters saying "God's People Are Rainbow People."*

Tell the participants they are all "Rainbow people." As members of God's family, God loves us. Through God's love, we can love God in return and we can love each other and work together.

Have the participants paint a colorful rainbow mural on a large sheet of paper. Then ask them to bring in photographs of themselves to add to the mural. You may decide to take the photographs yourself using an instant-developing camera. Make letters saying, "God's People Are Rainbow People" and put them above the rainbow.

World recipes (All ages). Have participants make foods from various countries. A recipe from Israel is given here. Choose a variety of recipes that will include simple things the youngest participants can make. Invite persons of various nationalities to prepare their favorite recipes.

Flat crackers
2 cups flour
1 teaspoon salt
½ teaspoon soda
¼ cup butter
½ cup sour milk (or ½ cup milk with 1 teaspoon vinegar added)
1 large egg
Sift flour, salt, and soda into a bowl. Cut the butter in until very fine. Add the milk and egg to make a stiff dough. Knead thoroughly and roll the dough very thin. Cut into squares or circles, and place on a lightly greased baking sheet. Pierce the crackers with a fork and bake in a 400 degree oven for 10 minutes or until lightly browned. Sprinkle with coarse salt if desired.

Storyteller (All ages). Ask an adult or teenager in your congregation to be a storyteller. There are many good books both in church and public libraries that would add to the theme of relationships.

Encourage the storyteller to tell, rather than read, the stories, if possible. Suggest that the storyteller dress as one of the characters in the story. Make a sign that tells the story title and time it will be told. Post it near the entrance to the Exploration Station.

Love cards (Preschool, lower elementary). *Materials needed: 9" x 12" sheets of white construction paper, felt-tip pen.*

Fold the paper into fourths, forming the card. Then let the participants design a rainbow on the outside of their cards. Write, or have the participants write, messages inside the cards, such as "God loves you," or "You are God's child." When the cards are completed, suggest that they be given to the pastor, who can deliver them to people in the hospital, in their homes, or in care facilities. We can show love to people we don't even know or see.

Kamishibai (kam-e-she-bi) storytellers (Elementary). *Materials needed: cardboard box, scissors or knife, self-adhesive paper or paint, construction paper, Bible, wooden craft sticks (optional).*

Cut a 9" high by 12" wide window in the side of a cardboard box. Turn the box upside down and cut a slit about 2" wide and 12" long in the bottom of the box, which is now turned upside down. Cover the box with self-adhesive paper or paint. Have the participants draw pictures on 9" x 12" construction paper that illustrate specific Bible stories. You may want to assign a particular story to a group of participants and have each one draw one scene from the story. To use the kamishibai, the story pictures are dropped through the slot in the top of the box and can be seen through the window in the front. If the box is quite large, the pictures may be fastened to wooden craft sticks in order to reach down far enough to be shown in the window. One person can tell the story as the pictures are shown.

Puppet people (All ages). As participants meet together, plan to use Bible stories and other contemporary stories they are familiar with to present puppet plays. Following are examples for making puppets:

Paper bag puppets. Participants enjoy making puppets using brown paper bags. These puppets are operated by inserting the hand into the bag and moving the folded over bottom of the bag like a "mouth" by flexing the knuckles. Use a variety of sizes, and have the participants incorporate fabric scraps, yarn, and paper to decorate their puppets.

Stocking-head puppets. Cut a 6" length of clean, used nylon stocking for each puppet head. Tie the top with thread, leaving about ½". Stuff the head with polyester filling, or small pieces of nylon stockings. Before tying off the bottom of the puppet, insert a craft stick.

Use embroidery thread to add facial features. Buttons can be sewn or glued on for the eyes. Use tiny stitches to outline the nose, mouth, and eyebrows. Use crayons to add color to the mouth and cheeks. Fake fur or yarn can be used for the puppet's hair.

To make simple clothing, cut a small slit in the center of a 16" cloth circle. Slip over the stick and tie a length of yarn around the waist.

"Oh, People Need Each Other" (All ages). Make up words to go with the tune of "Have You Ever Seen a Lassie." After writing the words, make a large song chart that can be posted and shared by all people visiting the center. Make simple rhythm instruments using aluminum cans, dowels, and wood blocks to accompany the song as you sing it. One example of words might be:

Oh, people need each other,
Each other, each other.
Oh, people need each other
'Cause people need love.

We can love each other,
Each other, each other.
We can love each other,
For God gives us love.

Community resource people (All ages). Invite a person involved with a care facility for the elderly to describe her or his job. If possible, have the person bring pictures and share stories about how love is experienced among people at the facility. Ask the person to suggest ways participants might be able to become involved in a volunteer project to help the facility.

Exchange table (All ages). People often express love for one another through gift giving. Encourage participants to bring old books, puzzles, toys, and games that they no longer use. Place these items on the exchange table for others to take home and use. Children should get permission from a parent and bring items that are in usable condition. At the end, all unclaimed items might be donated to a local community agency.

CARING KINGDOM

Theme: Caring for God's World

Objectives:
● to help participants become aware of God's gift of the world
● to teach participants how to care for the world

Setup: Make a large poster to identify this as the Caring Kingdom. Create another poster stating the theme for this area. Make three or four posters that deal with caring for the world to hang on the wall in the Caring Kingdom center. Write such things as, "This is God's world—take care of it" or "Caring for nature—you can make a difference." Paint foam balls to resemble globes and hang them from the ceiling or locate balloons or beach balls that are printed to represent the earth.

Draw a variety of animals and foliage on large sheets of paper. Cut out the animals and foliage shapes and attach them to a wall.

Collect dry weeds and flowers, arrange them in baskets or large brown paper bags (covered with shellac for a shiny finish), and place them throughout the room.

Label containers for recycling with labels such as "Aluminum," "Paper," or "Glass."

Make rainbow armbands for the guides to wear in the center. Write "Caring Kingdom" and the guide's name on the armband.

Caring Kingdom Activities

Rainbow gardens (All ages). *Materials needed: plant seeds, plant cuttings, egg cartons, individual-size milk cartons, or paper cups, markers, potting soil.*

As caretakers of God's world, plants and flowers are part of our responsibility. Collect plant seeds as well as plants that you can take cuttings from, such as Swedish ivy, philodendrons, and coleus. Using egg cartons, milk cartons, or paper cups, show the participants how to plant seeds in soil. Also show how to root plant cuttings in water.

Before the participants begin planting the seeds, have them decorate their containers in rainbow colors. After planting, place the containers on a tray. Keep each group's containers together on a tray to simplify the distribution of plants later.

Tree walk (Elementary, upper elementary). *Materials needed: leaves, large sheet of tagboard.*

Take a walk outside where you can find a variety of trees. Pick up leaves you find on the ground and bring them back to the center. Mount the leaves on a large sheet of tagboard.

Have books and reference materials available for the participants to research the leaves. Ask them to write facts and interesting information they find on the tagboard underneath the leaves. Hang the chart where everyone can see it.

Twig crosses (All ages). *Materials needed: twigs, driftwood, or small sticks, heavy twine or leather.*

Collect twigs, pieces of driftwood, or small sticks that are approximately the same diameter. A stick about 4"–6" is the best size. Using heavy twine or leather, lash two twigs together to form a cross. Wind the twine or leather several times around the intersection of the twigs, then tie a knot on the back and cut off the excess. This cross can be hung on the wall as a reminder of living in God's love every day.

Twig cross

"Care for Creation" wind chimes (Upper elementary). *Materials needed: juice can lids with a rolled edge (the type pulled off rather than cut with a can opener), construction paper, fine-tip markers, clear self-adhesive paper, scissors, a nail, a hammer, a block of wood, thin strips of wood approximately 1" wide by 8" long, fishing line, electric drill.*

Enlist an adult to drill a series of small holes along one edge of the wood strips. The number of holes will be determined by the number of lids you intend to provide for each participant. Try to have at least four.

Cut construction paper circles somewhat smaller in diameter than the flat surface of the lids. Cut an equal number of slightly larger circles from clear adhesive paper. One paper circle and one adhesive circle are needed for each lid used.

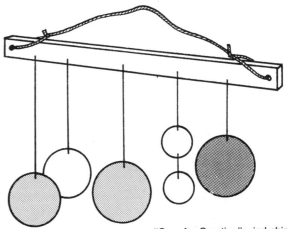

"Care for Creation" wind chime

Lead a discussion on the topic of endangered species and ecological concerns. Encourage the participants to write slogans or draw pictures on the construction paper circles that reflect concern for God's creation. Peel the backing from the clear self-adhesive paper and cover the paper circle. Apply the two circles to a lid, pressing the self-adhesive paper down to seal in the picture or slogan. Make a small hole in the top portion of each lid using a hammer and nail on a block of wood. Cut fishing line into various lengths and tie one end through the wood strip and the other through the hole in the lid. Position the lines so that the lids will touch one another and "chime" when moved by the wind.

Wise owl hanging (Elementary). *Materials needed: 4" x 8" pieces of gold felt or burlap, needles and thread, dowels, yarn, walnut shells, 2" twigs, doughnut-shaped oat cereal, small round pretzels, small pieces of brown felt, glue, fine-tip markers.*

Use the gold felt or burlap for the background. Fringe one end of the burlap and fold a 2" hem at the other end. Sew this hem, then slide a dowel or thin stick into it. Attach yarn for a hanger.

Using one half of a walnut shell, 2" twig or small piece of wood, oat cereal, two small round pretzels, and a small piece of brown felt, make an owl on the burlap as shown in the illustration. Glue the pieces on, allowing time for them to dry before adding any of the top pieces. Use a fine-tip marker to write the words, "Use God's Gifts Wisely."

Wise owl hanging

Dried weed collage (Elementary). *Materials needed: assorted colors of dried weeds and flowers, glue, 5" x 7" piece of cardboard, ribbon, clay dough, aluminum foil, oven, hook.*

Collect assorted colors of dried weeds and flowers. Glue the weeds to a 5" x 7" piece of cardboard. Attach a small piece of ribbon or trim to the weeds to look as if they are tied together.

Make clay dough from 4 cups flour, 1 cup salt, and 1¼ cups water. Add water gradually to the dry ingredients and mix thoroughly. Knead the mixture. Roll ropes of dough about the diameter of a pencil. Twist two ropes together and fit them around a 5" x 7" piece of cardboard like a frame. Slide the ropes from the cardboard onto a sheet of aluminum foil. Bake in a 325 degree oven for 15–20 minutes or until lightly brown. Glue the hardened clay frame onto the cardboard. Attach a hook for hanging.

"God's World" nature tag (Elementary). *Materials needed: 3" x 5" index cards, paper bag.*

Write the names or draw a picture of flowers, bushes, trees, and other nature objects you see in your church yard or a nearby park on 3" x 5" index cards. Print "It" on one index card, and put all the cards in a bag.

Take participants to the area. Point out the specific objects you have written down on the cards. Choose a home base for the tag game. Have the students reach into a bag of cards. The person who grabs the "It" card is "It" for the game. The other players will need to try to reach home base without being tagged.

The only way to be "safe" is to touch one of the objects identified on the index cards. "It" can ask the person touching the object what it is and how he or she can take care of it. If he or she answers correctly, the game continues as the participants try to reach home base. If he or she doesn't know the answer, he or she becomes "It." The game is finished when all players have safely reached home base.

Recycling center (All ages). Invite a person from the community or congregation who is involved in a recycling program to speak to the participants about what they can do to recycle. Talk to them about the amount of time and energy used to produce certain goods. Show the boxes you have prepared for recycling in the Caring Kingdom.

Encourage the participants to bring recyclable items from home to add to the boxes. Any money received when you turn the items into a recycling organization can be used for a special offering project. You may want to make a ballot box and let the participants vote on which project they would like to support.

Rolled magazine hot pad (Upper elementary). *Materials needed: colorful magazine pages, knitting needles, glue, scissors, thin cardboard.*

Carefully tear 25 colorful magazine pages from old magazines. Starting at one corner, with the colorful side facing down, roll each page tightly, diagonally around a knitting needle. Touch the corner with glue and remove the knitting needle. Cut the ends of the tube off so they are even. The tube should be the size of a fat straw. Glue the tubes side by side onto a thin sheet of cardboard. Trim to make a square.

PRAISE PLACE

Theme: Staying in Touch with God

Objectives:
● to help participants explore different ways to praise God
● to give participants opportunities to thank and praise God individually and with others

Setup: Make a large poster to identify this as the Praise Place. Create another poster stating the theme for this area. Prepare the sheets of chart paper required for "P-R-A-I-S-E" posters. Make a large chart of motions to accompany the Lord's Prayer and fasten it to the wall. Have a tape or a compact disc playing songs of praise.

Hang twisted crepe paper streamers and balloons from one wall to another wall or divider. Make rainbow armbands for the guides to wear in the center. Write "Praise Place" and the guide's name on the armband.

Praise Place Activities

"P-R-A-I-S-E" posters (All ages). *Materials needed: six large sheets of chart paper, markers, tape.*

On each of six sheets of chart paper, draw a large, colorful letter, so that together the posters form the word "PRAISE."

Discuss things for which the participants are thankful. Ask each one to think of words that begin with one of the letters on the posters. Invite them to write the name of or draw a picture of some of the things for which they are thankful, either from those suggested or of their own choosing. For example, under "I" someone might write or draw "ice cream," or under "P," parents. Encourage a variety of creative responses. Tape the posters on a wall or divider in Praise Place.

Community cheer (All ages). Write cheers that tell about living in God's love within the community of God's people. Have participants make up motions to the cheers as they learn them. Record the cheers on chart paper and mount them where others can see them. Have older participants teach the cheers to the younger groups. For example:
We live in God's love,
L-O-V-E.
We live in God's love,
We are free, free, free!

The Lord's Prayer (All ages). Make up motions for the Lord's Prayer like those suggested here. Use this prayer to give the participants new insights in the words of this well-known prayer.

Lord's Prayer motions

Celebration dance (Elementary). This dance may be performed with any number of participants. For music, use a joyful song with a four beat rhythm and 16 measures. Form a circle with the participants. Each one should stand beside a partner. Each step described below will take two measures, or eight beats.
1. Four claps.
2. Slide right four steps.
3. Four claps.
4. Slide left four steps.
5. Step forward (left foot first) two steps; stamp feet two times.
6. Step backward (right foot first) two steps; stamp feet two times.
7. Link arm with your partner; skip around in a complete circle.
8. Four claps.
Participants may wish to learn dance movements to other songs. Let them learn the movements and do the dances in the Praise Place.

Sing praise (All ages). Using the tune of "If You're Happy and You Know It," create a spirited song of praise. One verse might say: If you know that Jesus loves you, shout "Hurrah!" *(sung twice)*, if you really, really know it, then your life will surely show it. If you know that Jesus loves you, shout "Hurrah!" Compose other verses, perhaps incorporating body movements, such as stomping feet.

Praise psalm (Elementary). Invite the participants to take part in a praise psalm based on Psalm 112, Malachi 3:10, and 2 Corinthians 9. Select volunteers for the "Reader" parts. Divide the remaining students into two groups. On the chalkboard or chart paper print: "Group 1: Praise the Lord. Let all people praise the Lord." Separately, or on another sheet of paper, print: "Group 2: Happy are the people who love and obey God." The Group 1 and Group 2 responses are read first, then repeated after each "Reader" part. Signal each group when it is their turn.

Reader 1: They give generously to people who are needy, and their kindness never fails.

Reader 2: For God says, "Put me to the test and you will see that I will open the windows of heaven and pour out on you in abundance all kinds of good things."

Reader 3: For God loves the one who gives gladly. God will always make you rich enough to be generous at all times, so that many will thank God for your gifts.

Jump rope rhymes (Elementary, upper elementary). *Materials needed: jump ropes.*

Work together to develop jump rope rhymes, similar to those below, that exress praise to God.

God loves everybody! Ring the church bell!
Women, men, and children! How many can you tell? (*Count 1, 2, 3, 4. . . .*)

Thank God for the animals! Lion, snake, and bee!
On a visit to the zoo, how many do you see?
(*Count 1, 2, 3, 4. . . .*)

Rainbow of prayers (All ages). *Materials needed: copies of rainbow pattern, scissors, pens, pencils, crayons or markers, tape, yarn.*

On 8½" x 11" paper, draw a rainbow and clouds similar to the one shown here. Make photocopies of the pattern to supply each participant.

Invite the participants to color the rainbow, then cut around the top the curve and straight across the bottom from cloud to cloud. Talk about thanking God with our prayers. Ask each participant to use the space beneath the rainbow to write a short prayer giving thanks for one thing. Have the younger participants dictate their prayers to an adult, who will print their prayers for them. Tape the rainbows to the wall in the shape of a rainbow (a rainbow of rainbows). You may want to outline the large rainbow by taping colored yarn to the wall. Invite visitors to the center to read the thank-you prayers.

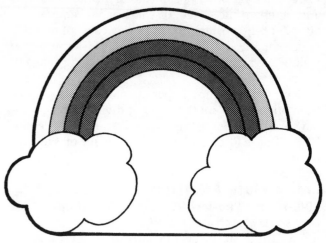

Rainbow of prayers

CRAFT RECIPES

The following are recipes for basic craft materials that can be implemented as additional or alternative activities in the learning centers. With some creative planning, they can be used in projects that reflect the various themes of the activity centers.

Baked craft dough
2 cups flour
1 cup salt
1 cup water

Mix and knead. Form into the desired shapes and transfer to a cookie sheet. Bake at 350 degrees for about 30 minutes or until golden. When hardened, paint with acrylic paints and spray with craft spray.

Cornstarch clay
2 cups salt
⅔ cup water
1 cup cornstarch
½ cup water
tempera paint or food coloring, if desired

Mix salt and ⅔ cup water in a pan over low heat, stirring constantly. When hot, remove from heat. Have the cornstarch and ½ cup water mixed and immediately add to the hot salt/water mixture. Stir rapidly; the mixture should become very thick. (Heat some more if it doesn't thicken.) Spoon the mixture onto a cookie sheet and cover with a wet cloth until cool. Knead the clay until smooth. Tempera paint or food coloring may be added to the salt and water mixture, if desired. Store in a plastic bag or airtight container.

Finger paint 1
1 envelope unflavored gelatin
¼ cup cold water
½ cup cornstarch
¾ cup cold water
2 cups boiling water
colorings: food coloring or fruit drink powder, soy sauce, mustard, spices

Add ¼ cup of water to gelatin and set aside. Mix ¾ cup water with cornstarch in saucepan. Stir boiling water and coloring into cornstarch. Cook over medium heat, stirring constantly, until mixture boils and becomes clear. Remove from heat and stir in gelatin mixture. Pour into jars with screw-on lids. Paint can be stored in tightly covered jars in the refrigerator for three to four days.

Finger paint 2
Mix equal part of liquid laundry starch and liquid tempera paint.

High gloss paint
Mix equal parts of liquid tempera paint and glue and use as a paint on clay or papier-mâché objects for a shiny effect. Store paint in an airtight container.

Puffy paint
½ cup flour
½ cup salt
½ cup water
liquid tempera paint
squares of cardboard
clean, empty plastic squeeze bottles such as those used for mustard or catsup

Mix the measured ingredients in a bowl, add the tempera paint, and stir. Pour into plastic squeeze bottles. Squeeze the contents onto the cardboard squares to create a design. Set the designs aside to air dry. They will retain a puffy surface.

Face paint
½ teaspoon water
½ teaspoon facial cold cream
½ teaspoon corn starch
a couple of drops of food coloring

Blend ingredients and apply.

Papier-mâché paste
1 cup flour
1 cup sugar
4 cups warm water
1 teaspoon powdered alum
few drops of oil of cloves

Mix dry ingredients in top of double boiler. Add water slowly, stirring constantly. After the paste has become clear, continue cooking for two more minutes. Remove from stove and add oil of cloves, mixing well. Keep in airtight containers. Thin when necessary by adding small amounts of water. Makes one quart.

Playdough 1
1 cup flour
1 cup water
1 tablespoon oil
1 tablespoon alum
½ cup salt
2 tablespoons vanilla (optional)
food coloring, if desired

Mix all of the dry ingredients. Add oil and water. Cook on medium heat. Stir constantly until it reaches the consistency of mashed potatoes. Remove from heat. Add vanilla and food coloring if you wish. Divide into balls and knead to mix in the coloring. Store in an airtight container or plastic bag.

Playdough 2
6 cups flour
1 cup salt
1 tablespoon alum (added to the flour before adding water)
1 tablespoon cooking oil
2 or 3 cups lukewarm water
food coloring added to the water

Add the liquids slowly to the dry ingredients and knead. Store in tightly sealed plastic bag to keep indefinitely.

"Sandy" playdough
1 cup sand
½ cup cornstarch
1 teaspoon powdered alum
¾ cup hot water
food coloring (optional)

Mix the dry ingredients together. Add the liquids and cook over medium heat until thick, stirring constantly. Makes about two cups. Roll into balls of desired size, then flatten or roll out to ½" thickness. Cut into shapes if desired. Make imprints with various objects. Leave to dry in the open air for several days.

Soapsuds paint
1 cup powdered detergent
5 tablespoons liquid starch
food coloring, if desired

Mix detergent and starch. Beat with a rotary beater until the mixture is the consistency of frosting. Add coloring if desired. Add water as needed.

FOOD IDEAS AND PRAYERS

Food Ideas

Food is always a welcome part of fellowship times. The following recipes can be used to prepare food for the group ahead of time, or prepared with the participants as additional or alternative learning center activities.

Bible-times bread
3½ to 4 cups flour (one half of the flour used may be whole wheat)
2 teaspoons salt
1 package active dry yeast
1½ cups very warm tap water
butter

Mix thoroughly 1 cup of the flour, the salt, and the undissolved yeast in a large bowl. Gradually add the warm water to the dry ingredients and beat. Add ¾ cup flour and mix well.

Stir in enough additional flour to make a stiff dough. Turn out onto a lightly floured board and knead about 5 minutes, until smooth and elastic. Divide dough into eight equal pieces, cover, and let rest for at least 15 minutes.

Roll each piece into a 5" circle on a lightly floured board. Place the circles on greased baking sheets and brush with melted butter. Let rise for 45 minutes, then bake at 500 degrees for 10 minutes or until lightly browned. Cool on racks.

Cereal snack mix
2 cups wheat square cereal
2 cups corn square cereal
2 cups rice square cereal
1½ cups mixed nuts
6 tablespoons butter or margarine
4 teaspoons Worcestershire sauce
1 teaspoon seasoned salt

Melt butter and add Worcestershire sauce and salt. Pour butter mixture over dry ingredients and stir. Heat in oven at 200 degrees for about 30 minutes, stirring the mixture every 10 minutes. Makes 7½ cups. If an oven is not available, use an electric fry pan.

Middle Eastern candy
2 cups pitted dates
2 cups walnuts
butter
powdered sugar

Chop dates and nuts very finely. Mix the dates and nuts together, rubbing with the back of a spoon until smooth. Spread the creamed date-nut mixture about ½" thick on a buttered plate. Let dry; cut into small squares or diamonds. Sprinkle with powdered sugar.

Flat bread
1½ cups white flour
½ cup whole wheat flour
1 teaspoon salt
¾ teaspoon baking soda
2 tablespoons shortening
½ cup water
1½ teaspoons honey

Mix together the white flour, whole wheat flour, salt, and baking soda. Add the shortening to the mixture, and cut in. Gradually add the water mixed with the honey, until the mixture forms a ball. Divide the dough into four parts and knead. Roll each part into a circle ⅜" thick. Place the circles on a lightly greased cookie sheet. Use a fork to score the surface of each circle into bite-sized pieces, taking care not to cut through the dough. Bake for 10 minutes at 350 degrees. Use a fork to prick any air bubbles that form as the bread bakes. After the bread has cooled, spread it with honey or butter, break it into pieces, and enjoy.

Homemade butter
1 pint whipping cream at room temperature
salt

Pour whipping cream into a quart jar and screw the lid on tightly. Pass the jar from person to person, giving each one an opportunity to shake the jar for a few minutes. The time required for the cream to turn into a ball of butter can vary, but usually occurs in 15–30 minutes. Pour off the excess buttermilk and salt lightly.

Honey butter
½ cup honey
½ cup softened butter or margarine

Whip the butter with an egg beater or mixer. Add honey and continue to beat until thoroughly mixed. Use as a spread on bread or crackers.

Cookie dough
1 cup brown sugar
1 cup white sugar
1 cup shortening
4 cups flour
1 teaspoon baking soda
1 tablespoon cinnamon
3 eggs
1 teaspoon salt

Cream the shortening in a mixer; add the sugars; mix; add eggs and mix again. Mix the dry ingredients and add to the creamed mixture. Chill the dough until ready to bake.

Fruit shake
2 cups milk
1 teaspoon vanilla
4 to 8 ice cubes
2 bananas or 2 cups strawberries, peaches, or other fresh fruit
1 or 2 tablespoons honey or sugar (optional)

Whirl ingredients together in a blender. Sweeten with honey or sugar if desired. Makes 1 quart.

Applesauce
one apple per participant
water
sugar (approximately 1 tablespoon per apple)
cinnamon

Peel, core, and slice apples and place in a large saucepan. Add water to cover by 2". Add sugar to taste and sprinkle with cinnamon. Bring to a boil and stir constantly until apples are soft and can be mashed together. Eat warm or cold.

Snack mix
granola
peanuts
coconut
dried fruit
raisins

Mix ingredients together in any proportion. Serve this snack in a cup or by the handful.

Peanut butter granola
2 tablespoons corn oil
⅓ cup peanut butter
¼ cup brown sugar
2½ cups rolled oats
½ cup raisins

Stir corn oil into peanut butter, then stir in sugar. Add oats and stir until well mixed. Spread on baking sheet and bake at 300 degrees. Stir occasionally. Bake 15 to 20 minutes or until lightly browned. Remove from oven and add raisins.

Soft whole wheat pretzels
2 (16-oz.) loaves frozen whole wheat bread dough, thawed
1 egg white, slightly beaten
1 teaspoon water
coarse salt

Thaw bread in the refrigerator overnight. From each loaf shape 12 1½" balls. Roll each ball into a rope approximately 14" long. Shape into pretzels by forming a knot and looping ends through. Arrange pretzels 1" apart on well-greased baking sheet. Let stand for 20 minutes. Brush combined egg white and water on pretzels, then sprinkle with coarse salt. Place a shallow pan containing 1" of boiling water on a lower rack in the oven. Bake pretzels on a cookie sheet on a rack above the water at 350 degrees for 20 minutes or until golden brown. Makes two dozen pretzels.

Taffy pull
1 cup sugar
1 tablespoon cornstarch
¾ cup light corn syrup
⅔ cup water
2 tablespoons margarine or butter
1 teaspoon salt
saucepan
2 teaspoons vanilla or almond extract
8" x 8" baking pan
candy thermometer
waxed paper
scissors
brown bags

Butter pan. Mix sugar and cornstarch in saucepan. Stir in light corn syrup, water, margarine or butter, and salt. Heat to boiling over medium heat, stirring constantly. Cook without stirring to 256 degrees on candy thermometer, about 30 minutes. Watch mixture very carefully. Remove pan from heat. Stir in vanilla or almond extract. Pour into 8" x 8" baking pan. Makes about 5 dozen pieces.

Make the taffy about 45 minutes before the participants arrive. Have them wash their hands thoroughly. Seated with a partner, each pair should have waxed paper and scissors. When taffy is just cool enough to handle, the participants need to begin pulling the candy with lightly buttered hands until taffy is satiny and stiff. At this point, one partner should pull the taffy into strips about ½" wide. The other partner needs to begin cutting waxed paper into 2" x 4" pieces. Break the taffy into pieces 1" long and wrap in the waxed paper, twisting the ends of the paper. Have participants divide up their taffy pieces evenly. Provide bags for taking home the taffy.

Make-a-face cakes
rice cakes
peanut butter
raisins
apple slices
banana slices

Spread peanut butter on the rice cake. Add raisins for eyes, a banana slice for a nose, and an apple slice for the mouth. Eat!

Friends fruit salad
Each participant brings in one piece of fresh fruit. Peel the fruit and cut into chunks with a table knife. Mix the fruit chunks together. Sprinkle on a little lemon juice. Sugar is optional. Chill and enjoy the snack together.

Fruit juice on a stick
Freeze juice in small paper cups, inserting a wood craft stick or a small plastic spoon for a handle just before it freezes. Peel away the cups when ready to eat.

Partner ice cream
1 three-pound coffee can, with plastic lid
1 cup whipping cream
½ cup sugar
1 teaspoon vanilla
1 one-pound coffee can, with plastic lid
1 cup whole milk
1 egg (beaten)
¾ cup rock salt
ice

Place the mixture, except the rock salt and ice, in the one-pound can, and seal tightly. Wrap the can in a thin plastic bag or plastic wrap. Place this can inside the three-pound can. Add ice to fill and ½ to ¾ cup of rock salt to the larger can and seal tightly. Lay the can on its side and have pairs of participants take turns rolling it back and forth to one another on a tabletop for 20 to 25 minutes. Makes four cups.

Individual pudding cups
Give each participant one tablespoon of instant pudding and three tablespoons of milk in a jar with a tight-fitting lid. Have everyone shake their jars until the pudding thickens. Eat with a spoon directly from the jar.

No-bake peanut butter balls
½ cup peanut butter
2½ tablespoons nonfat dry milk
2 tablespoons raisins
2 tablespoons honey
¼ cup coconut

Mix and roll into walnut-sized balls.

Fruit gelatin
½ cup sugar
4 envelopes unflavored gelatin
2½ cups fruit juice (pineapple, orange, grape, or apple)

Mix sugar and gelatin in mixing bowl. Bring fruit juice to a boil. Pour hot juice over gelatin and sugar mixture. Stir until dissolved. Pour into a 13" x 9" x 2" pan. Chill until firm. Cut into squares. Eat with your fingers.

Prayers
Give thanks for the food, using one of the following prayers or one of your own.

God is great, God is good. Let us thank God for our food. Amen.

Come, Lord Jesus, be our guest and let these gifts to us be blessed. Amen.

We fold our hands and bow our heads and thank you for our daily bread. Amen.

For health and strength and daily food we praise your name, oh Lord. Amen.

NOTES